About
The Si✖ties

About
The Si❌ties

DISCARDED

by "The Usual Gang of Idiots"

Quality Paperback Book Club
New York

To William M. Gaines:

"FUN AROUND THE CLOCK YOU BET WE HAD OUR FILL!"

—"The Usual Gang of Idiots"

Compiled and preliminary design by Grant Geissman

Special thanks to:

Charles Kochman and Sandy Resnick (DC Comics),

Nick Meglin, John Ficarra, and Joe Orlando (MAD Magazine),

Greg Tobin (QPB) and Les Pockell (Book-of-the-Month Club),

Mark Chimsky, Clif Gaskill, and Caroline Hagen (Little, Brown),

Ian Ballantine (the visionary who published

the first MAD reprints in paperback form),

and especially the talented writers, artists, editors, and

conspirators who have rotted the minds of MAD readers for five decades.

I began reading **MAD** in **1961** after being turned on to the magazine by some older and wiser neighborhood kids. Having been weaned on milder fare like Superman and Batman comic books, I was amazed that such an outrageous magazine could exist, and even more amazed that it was readily available to an eight-year-old such as myself. I loved **MAD**; we all did. We bought every issue, devoured it, and discussed what we had read and seen within its pages. A few of us even had subscriptions and sent away for the pictures of Alfred E. Neuman that were advertised for a quarter. We knew the names of the artists and writers, the name of publisher William M. Gaines, and some of the more fanatical among us could even recite the names of its editors and production staff without knowing exactly what it was that they did. One name thus committed to memory, Nick Meglin, has appeared on the masthead of every issue for about thirty-nine years now. Of course, at the time I got hooked on **MAD** I had no idea that it would become a lifelong obsession with me. . . .

Nick Meglin: You? What about me, fella? You I think I planned it that my first professional full-time job, which I regarded as only a temporary position, would become my lifelong obsession?

Not if you say so. Where was I? Oh yeah . . . nor did I have the slightest idea that I would actually get to know many of "the usual gang of idiots." What would have been even more incredible to my younger self is that I would now be writing an introduction to a book containing material that I first read then, and that my introduction would be interrupted by an original member of the "idiot gang."

N.M.: Think nothing of it, my good man. I'm honored to do so.

Excellent. Can I go on now?

Although **MAD** was born in the **1950s**, it was in the **1960s** that the magazine came of age. The decade began quietly enough as a continuation of the Eisenhower fifties, but this proved to be just the calm before the storm. The sixties would bring, among other things, protest singers, an escalating Vietnam war, a new but altogether different invasion by the British, hippies, sit-ins, slogans ("Make Love Not War," "Flower Power"), Pop Art, and the Generation Gap, almost all of which served as prime fodder for the **MAD** satirists. The **MAD** message, almost from its inception, was not to believe everything you see, that authority might need to be questioned sometimes, and that absurdity abounds—a message that was not lost on its readers. By the end of the **1960s**, **MAD** found itself in the position of not only being able to comment on the changing scene, but also of having played a part in causing those changes. If the sixties came in like a lamb and went out like a lion, then **MAD**—which always came in like a lion—had by the end of the decade grown a new set of bigger and even sharper feline teeth and been provided with a staggering number of lambs for the satirical slaughter.

N.M.: That MAD "rotted minds" becomes obvious when I read evidence of gray matter decay in words like the preceding. "Satirical slaughter" indeed. Hey, all we were doing was having fun. As a veteran of the trenches I assure you there wasn't a day when we took ourselves seriously, which probably explains why we're still around and over a hundred wannabes that surfaced through the years aren't. Pretension was always our target, never our frailty. Hmm, did that sound pretentious?

Ahem, well, a bit.

MAD began in the fall of 1952 as a ten-cent comic book published by William M. Gaines's EC Comics group and written entirely by Harvey Kurtzman. The first issue looked little farther than Gaines's own horror and science fiction comics (*Tales from the Crypt, Weird Science,* et al.) for its objects of parody. The second and third issues consisted mostly of "probing fire" at none-too-clearly-defined satirical targets. The fourth issue, however, carried a brilliant parody of Superman ("Superduperman"), and the die was cast. Comic books, comic strips, movies, television shows, literature, and various aspects of modern living became grist for the MAD mill. MAD was a success, but after nearly three years and twenty-three comic book issues, Kurtzman, who had always wanted to try his hand at slick magazines, convinced Gaines to let him reinvent MAD as a twenty-five-cent magazine. This first magazine (issue #24) appeared in July 1955 and flew off the newsstands, prompting Gaines to go back to press for extra copies—an unheard-of practice in magazine publishing. Converting MAD to a magazine proved to be an almost miraculous bit of serendipity, for Gaines's horror and crime comic books were rapidly being forced out of business by vociferous and reactionary civic leaders and politicians who had become convinced that such comic books were the cause of juvenile delinquency.

N.M.: One of my earliest articles for MAD lampooned Dr. Frederick Wertham, a child psychologist who, armed with his book Seduction of the Innocent, *became the vanguard of a small but high-profile movement espousing comic books as the primary cause of juvenile delinquency—a movement that ultimately drove Gaines's comic books out of business. The article "Baseball Is Ruining Our Children" (MAD*

#34, July–August 1957) broadly presented "Dr. Frederick Worthless's" evidence that since all juvenile delinquents have been exposed to baseball, this must be the cause of juvenile delinquency. The parallel absurdity of this "cause and effect" should have escaped no one.

By 1956, all that remained of Gaines's publishing empire was MAD. After Kurtzman had produced five magazine issues of MAD he found that he had also attracted the attention of a young Hugh Hefner, who had achieved phenomenal success by starting *Playboy* magazine several years earlier. Hefner made Kurtzman an offer that must have seemed like the chance of a lifetime: to take the concept Kurtzman started in MAD and flesh it out with more risqué subject matter and a big budget, printing in full color on expensive, slick paper. With Hefner's offer in his back pocket, Kurtzman went to Gaines and demanded 51 percent of MAD. Gaines refused, and Kurtzman walked, taking with him most of MAD's artists. Gaines was distraught, convinced that MAD could not continue without Kurtzman. On the advice of close friend Lyle Stuart, Gaines enlisted Al Feldstein to take the editorial helm. Feldstein had been heavily involved with Gaines's horror, science fiction, and crime comics and had found himself an unemployed casualty of their demise. Feldstein came aboard with issue twenty-nine (September 1956).

Shortly thereafter, the public-domain face of a grinning idiot boy that Kurtzman had peppered through the magazine under various names was married together for all time with the name Alfred E. Neuman.

N.M.: There was a brief moment when Alfred was considered dispensable. After starring on two successful covers (we ran him for President on issue #30; he was enshrined on Mt. Rushmore on issue #31), I argued that we had in Alfred the equivalent of Playboy's *Rabbit,* Esquire's *Esky, and* The New Yorker's *Whatsisface. Gaines challenged: "If you want to keep him on the cover, come up with five good Alfred cover ideas by tomorrow morning and I'll consider it." That night I loaded the deck. Knowing Bill's interest in and enthusiasm for ancient Egypt, I topped my five offerings with an ancient Egyptian tomb idea. "I love it," he chuckled, and the Egyptian tomb cover of #32 marked the issue in which Alfred became the official mascot. He has graced the cover of almost every issue since.*

Little by little, a new team of staffers was put into place, including a young writer named Nick Meglin (listed on the masthead under "ideas"), who helped Feldstein gather together a new group of freelance artists and writers. Among the new artists: Don Martin, Mort Drucker, Norman Mingo, Kelly Freas, Dave Berg, Bob Clarke, George Woodbridge, and later Antonio Prohias, Paul Coker, Sergio Aragonés, and Jack Rickard. Returning veterans were Wallace Wood (who maintained a working relationship with both Kurtzman and MAD) and Joe Orlando, who had worked on Gaines's EC comics. New writers included Frank Jacobs, Tom Koch, Arnie Kogen, Gary Belkin, Sy Reit, Larry Siegel, and later Phil Hahn, Stan Hart, and Dick De Bartolo. Jacobs would go on to become MAD's Poet Laureate and one of its most prolific contributors. Kogen, Belkin, Hahn, Siegel, and Hart would go on not only to work for MAD but also to do highly regarded (and sometimes Emmy Award–winning) work in television. Art director John Putnam (who had worked on Kurtzman's MAD and was the only full-time staffer who remained after Kurtzman's departure) was something of an unsung hero: possessed of an encyclopedic knowledge of typefaces and a quirky artistic sensibility, Putnam added the final typographic design to the magazine's parodies.

N.M.: The term "the usual gang of idiots" has endured as the self-imposed name of the team comprised of the handful of stars whose divergent talents and personalities fortunately blended into a solid unit. Of us all, I've always felt that John Putnam received far too little acknowledgment for his outstanding contribution to MAD's success. He was a quiet, gentle man, intellectually brilliant, culturally sophisticated, and creatively understated. As much as he was a perfectionist on the printed page, John's unkempt appearance rivaled only that of Bill Gaines. But unlike his beloved boss, his dishevelment was not limited to his wardrobe (Gaines was anal-retentive dealing with his papers, wines, and various collections), and we were always amazed that such a precise layout could emerge from John's drawing table, surviving the spills of today's olives, yesterday's salami, and tomorrow's sardines—not to mention the paints and glue he used for his model military figures. Sometimes just finding the final pasted-up pages under the stacks of French poetry books and strewn issues of The Realist *(for which Putnam wrote a sardonic column for many years) became a morning's work.*

By about 1958, MAD was selling a million copies a month, and by the dawn of the 1960s, the magazine was regarded by many as a national treasure and by some as a national disgrace. Gaines, after being vilified for his horror comics and abandoned by Harvey Kurtzman, had emerged triumphant. He began to reward his staffers and the freelancers who had met a minimum yearly page count by taking them on lavish, all-expense-paid group trips to exotic locales.

N.M.: The MAD trips serve as the best example of Bill Gaines's ability to provide a context for creativity and unity while at the same time rewarding his loyal band with incentives unheard-of in this freelance-oriented profession. Artists and writers joined the staffers in these yearly sojourns, which were also attended by MAD's legal and accounting teams as well as various others who had contributed to the magazine's success in that particular year. For instance, before he had achieved worldwide fame as the author of Ragtime *and other award-winning literature, E. L. Doctorow edited MAD's first four paperback anthologies (published by Ian Ballantine) and thus found himself trekking Virgin Island beaches with Gaines and his motley crew. Starting with modest trips to the Caribbean, the list soon included Mexico, South America, England, France, Italy, Spain, Russia, Greece, Germany, Morocco, Austria, Switzerland, Denmark, Africa, Tahiti, Japan, and more. Perhaps MAD's greatest achievement remains that not one of these countries broke off diplomatic relations with the U.S.A. after a MAD invasion of their soil.*

Illustration by Wallace Wood/MAD #68, January 1962

Daddy is a crook, child! He publishes MAD Magazine!

A large, gruff-but-affable man with a paternal nature, Gaines had an unusual policy regarding office deportment: as long as the work got done, the deadlines were met, and the magazine made money, he didn't care how long the lunch hours were, about the staff punching a time clock, or about any certain code of dress. Paradoxically, Gaines was also as cheap as he could be generous and on one notorious occasion stopped work in the office for two days to track down a personal long-distance phone call no one would admit to. As a lark, he once filled up the office water cooler with wine and spent the day watching his staff get even nuttier than usual. "I create the atmosphere, the staff creates the magazine," said Gaines, in perfect summation. By the early 1970s Bill Gaines had come to be regarded as one of the world's great eccentrics, and by the time of his death in 1992 he had become a full-blown American cultural icon. Space prohibits an in-depth celebration of the man, but fortunately there are several books about Gaines and the unique history of MAD: *The MAD World of William M. Gaines* by Frank Jacobs in 1972, *Completely MAD* by Maria Reidelbach in 1991, and *Good Days and MAD* by Dick DeBartolo in 1994.

The MAD experience can be many things to many people. "MAD doesn't really create as much as reflect," says Nick Meglin. "We hold a fun house mirror up to life." But that's not the whole story. To us kids in the early sixties, MAD provided not just a fun house mirror but a two-way mirror into the *real* world, a world MAD-ly skewed, but one that would be unfathomable *without* MAD. What kept us buying the magazine (when the same money would have netted two comic books and a candy bar) was that MAD was a sort of first primer for adult life, a necessary ingredient and manual for the rites of passage. How many preteens, for example, would have seen films like *Lawrence of*

Arabia or TV shows like *Peyton Place*, or would have read books like *Lolita* or *The Tropic of Cancer* (both subjects of paperback book cover satires)? How many would have known all the political figures in MAD articles like "A Day with J.F.K." or "East Side Story" without MAD as the point of reference? We not only laughed at MAD, we gleaned from it things we never could have gotten from our school textbooks and learned by default things that we otherwise would not have cared to know (and all for a mere 25¢—cheap!). Because the MAD staff produced a magazine that they themselves enjoyed, MAD's humor had several layers.

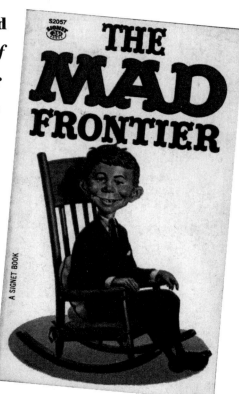

Some of the humor was aimed right down at our level where we could get at it, but, tantalizingly, much of it was a bit beyond us, which made the magazine all the more indispensable. When all was said and done, the really boss, tough, and bitchin' thing about MAD was that it *was* a magazine for adults (with a readership that extended from us to high school, college, and far beyond), but we "got it" too, and the guy in the drugstore didn't look at you funny if you tried to buy a copy.

N.M.: It's interesting to note that . . .

You again? Whose intro is this supposed to be, anyway?

N.M.: What do you know? You were just a kid when we were doing the stuff you're now waxing so poetically about! Have you written even one article for the magazine? Drawn one line of artwork? Well, have you, boomer boy?

(Humbled) Sorry, Mr. Meglin, sir. Please do go on with your enlightening commentary.

Any discussion of what **MAD** is merits a discussion of what **MAD** is not. **MAD** is not now, nor has it ever been, mean-spirited. Some people (usually one's parents) may argue that **MAD** is in questionable taste, but that is a subjective argument at best. Although it may not appear so to the casual observer, there is a line **MAD** will not cross. You *won't* find in **MAD**, for example, pieces like "The Lighter Side of the Manson Family," "A **MAD** Look at Assassinations," or "A **MAD** Peek Behind the Scenes at the Watts Riots." Furthermore, **MAD** has never shown a marked preference for either political party, although most of the staffers are self-avowed liberals. Being only human, members of both parties are equally apt to do idiotic things and therefore to leave themselves open to get the **MAD** treatment. **MAD** poked a fair amount of fun at John Kennedy, for instance, until his assassination brought a tragic end to the New Frontier. Out of respect, the cover to *The MAD Frontier* paperback (with Alfred E. Neuman in Kennedy's beloved rocking chair) was changed to a more generic one. No mention was made in **MAD** about the tragedy, and no further parodies of John (or Jackie) Kennedy were ever done.

As the sixties wore on and became The Sixties, profound and unprecedented changes were taking place. The Baby Boom generation was coming of age and consequently the youth of America had become empowered as never before. As Mods turned to Hippies and Hippies turned to Yippies, the **MAD**-men were there with pens in hand—no stoner was left unturned. Didn't this amount to biting the hand that feeds you? "Maybe it's not good business, but it's good **MAD**" was the typical Bill Gainesian reply. Just how right he was became clear in selecting the material for this book; it was not a matter of deciding what to put in, but rather of agonizing over what had to be left out.

N.M.: Who could have known that Time *magazine's early appraisal of MAD as a "short-lived satirical pulp" would be so utterly inaccurate, and that that "satirical pulp" would one day become a part of their magazine empire? Hah? Who? Hoohah!*

Who let him in here, anyway?

Students of history who might want to get a feel for the mores, attitudes, pop culture, and politics of the sixties could do far worse than to study the material herein, because the tenor of the times is all there, albeit seen through the eyes of "the usual gang of idiots."

So, if you lived through the sixties but can't remember them, or if you missed the sixties but wish you hadn't, join us for a MAD look at this Jabberwocky decade—a trip far stranger than even Jerry Garcia could have imagined.

—Grant Geissman, as interrupted by Nick Meglin

GRANT GEISSMAN is the author of *Collectibly MAD—the MAD and EC Collectibles Guide* (Kitchen Sink Press, 1995). Unfortunately, he has plans for other book projects.

What is this thing called MAD? It is, for one thing, an example of a whole that is greater than the sum of its parts. Which is not to imply that its parts are so shabby, either. The magazine has been fortunate to be able to draw upon a pool of absolutely world-class creative talent, people who also happened to be world-class misfits. Was the resulting *oeuvre* a catalyst for, or merely a reaction to, the tumultuous series of events encapsulated within, for example, the period of history we now refer to as "the sixties"? Who knows? Who cares? Least of all MAD's "usual gang of idiots"!

January 1960: Dwight D. Eisenhower is winding down his second term in the White House, the number one song in the country is "El Paso" by Marty Robbins, and the *new* little MAD family has been turning out the magazine for just over three years.

John Kennedy and Richard Nixon were gearing up for their respective campaigns in the upcoming presidential race. As you will discover, MAD had their own candidate in mind and threw Alfred E. Neuman's hat into the ring with the cover of issue #56 (July 1960); Kennedy, Nixon, Humphrey, Rockefeller, Truman, Eisenhower, and Johnson appear holding Alfred's placards. When the November election was held the race was considered too close to call, so MAD ran a double-sided cover on issue #60 (January 1961, but actually on the newsstands the previous November): one side congratulated Kennedy and the other congratulated Nixon. Kennedy also made the cover several issues after the election, with Alfred appearing as a press conference reporter from hell.

The "dog and totem pole" cover of issue #74 (October 1962) was the last cover done by Kelly Freas for MAD. Freas, who in addition to his MAD work was also a highly respected and Hugo Award–winning science fiction illustrator, felt he was getting a little stale doing Alfred and declined further work.

After a nearly five-year absence, Norman Mingo returned as MAD's cover artist. So great was the audience recognition factor to the magazine that Mingo's cover for issue #76 (January 1963) could feature a wildly distorted MAD logo; cover boy Alfred appears in rear view as well. The Mingo cover for issue #80 (July 1963) was the first use of a "panel gag" (sequential panels leading to a punch line) on a cover. Incidentally, Mingo's costuming of Alfred during this period makes him quite a bit younger than the earlier Freas version, more of an older boy than a young adult. In the years following, Alfred bounced back and forth between younger and older as the subject matter required: old enough for a shotgun wedding or young enough to ride in a baby carriage (the *Rosemary's Baby* movie satire).

Freas illustrated not only MAD's covers but also many ad parodies. MAD has never accepted paid advertising, so they were able to freely satirize any product's ad campaign without fear of retribution (the kind that hits other magazines hardest: loss of ad revenue). Freas's "Eastzone Kossak Company" ad was no doubt inspired by the U.S. trip made by Russia's Premier Khrushchev in October 1959. Khrushchev visited Hollywood, but security officials felt it was too dangerous for him to tour Disneyland. "Do you have rocket launching pads there?" Khrushchev angrily queried. MAD's ad has "tourist" Khrushchev using "Kossacolor" film in his camera. In true cold war spirit, if there *had* been rocket launching pads in Disneyland, Khrushchev would surely have tried to photograph them.

Curiously, the departure of Freas from MAD's pages roughly coincided with the end of the golden age of magazine illustration. By around the end of 1963, Madison Avenue's medium for its message became photography, not illustration. The "What Sort of Man Reads MAD?" photo ad is a takeoff on similar self-aggrandizing ads *Playboy* was running at the time. Appearing in the "Sucka Instant Coffee" ad is staffer Nick Meglin as the coffee grower. Staffers often played parts in MAD's photo parodies. Professional models were often unable or unwilling to pull the kinds of faces the parodies required, and the MAD-men found they could do it faster and better on their own. Other staff appearances: Jerry De Fuccio in the "What Sort of Man . . ." ad, Meglin and writer Frank Jacobs (in drag) in the "Do blondes have more fun?" parody, Meglin (trooper) and Al Feldstein (driver) in the "State Trooper/Texaco" parody, and production man Lenny Brenner in the "S'matter, can't you Dial?" ad.

"The MAD Madison Avenue Primer" is only the second "primer" (MAD's adult version of a children's schoolbook) the magazine did. Madison Avenue, and the advertising propaganda the agencies that were housed there turned out, was the source for much of MAD's humor. Another piece with a Madison Avenue theme, "My Fair Ad-man," is the first musical parody ever to appear in MAD and one of the few bylined pieces penned by Private Nick Meglin (who was then serving the last six months of his two-year U.S. Army draft requirement). Cary Grant, who became the archetypal ad man in Alfred Hitchcock's classic *North by Northwest*, appears as the "Higgenbottom" character. A goateed and bereted Frank Sinatra appears as the beatnik writer Irving Mallion.

"If Comic Book Characters Were as Old as Their Strips" is one of MAD's best-remembered premises. Rendered with a forger's eye by Wallace Wood, the piece was written by Earle Doud, who was enjoying great success at the time with a series of very MAD-like albums parodying the Kennedy family (*The First Family*, *The First Family Rides Again*). The charming "A Day with J.F.K." piece (MAD #67, December 1961), by Larry Siegel and Mort Drucker, is actually a spiritual cousin to Doud's *First Family* albums. Doud's work for MAD was part of a cross-pollination that was taking place: several MAD writers, including Larry Siegel, Frank Jacobs, Dick DeBartolo, and Nick Meglin, also worked on some Doud-produced comedy albums. The other Earle Doud piece appearing here is "Bananaz," MAD's parody of *Bonanza*. *Bonanza* is regarded by many as *the* TV western of the sixties and was the number one show from 1964 to 1967.

"East Side Story" is Frank Jacobs's and Mort Drucker's tour de force *West Side Story*/United Nations musical parody. Jacobs's parody lyrics fit seamlessly into the Leonard Bernstein melodies they were based upon. Drucker by this time was regarded by many as the country's best caricaturist. Apropos of his MAD political caricatures, he would later do several covers for *Time* magazine featuring political figures (as did Jack Davis).

Don Martin ("MAD's maddest artist") contributed his only sixties-era MAD cover on the January 1962 issue: the wonderful painting of the hinge-toed fighting Santas. Most of Don's work appeared in black and white. The page appearing in this section, "In a 'Greasy Spoon' Diner," is a good example of early Don Martin: pre–sound effects, and looser and more kinetic than his later work. The subject matter also tended to fall into the category of what was then termed "sick" humor.

Artist Antonio Prohias fled Castro's Cuba several days before Castro took over Cuba's free press. Prohias was one of Cuba's most influential political cartoonists, but his anti-Communist cartoons had made him persona non grata with the Castro regime. He arrived in New York with little else but his talent. Once there, Prohias labored in a clothing factory in Queens for several months while putting together a portfolio of new material, and when he was finished he headed for MAD. One of the ideas he showed was "SPY vs SPY," which became one of MAD's best-known features. The strip that appears in this section is the very first to appear, from MAD #60 (January 1961). The other Prohias piece in this section, "Vengeance," is a sublime example of the pantomime cartoon and one of the few non–"SPY vs SPY" pieces Prohias ever did for MAD.

In 1962, Spanish-born (but Mexico City–raised) artist Sergio Aragonés arrived in New York's Greenwich Village, where he found work as a singing waiter. What he really wanted, however, was to work for MAD. And like Prohias before him, Aragonés worked up some samples and headed for the MAD office. Upon showing his wares, Sergio was stunned by the fact that the MAD editors bought material literally out of his portfolio. He was further stunned to get a check from Bill Gaines on the spot. "A MAD Look at the U.S. Space Effort" is Sergio's first two-page article and was among the work MAD purchased that day. Incredibly fast on the draw, Sergio has often kept fellow diners spellbound by creating amazingly detailed tableaux on tablecloths and napkins.

"If Kids Designed Their Own Xmas Toys" is one of the most ingenious pieces ever to appear in MAD. The article was written and drawn by Al Jaffee, who also built the models. Jaffee was one of the original MAD magazine artists who had departed with Harvey Kurtzman for browner pastures. Jaffee was back in the fold by 1963 and would go on to create many of MAD's best-loved features.

Ending this section is "The Parting Shot," illustrated by Joe Orlando. This was one of Bill Gaines's favorite pieces in MAD, so when the MAD art was being auctioned in the late 1980s his wife Annie bought him the page as a gift. Annie recalls that she and Bill had a deal that whoever died first would be "last-tagged" by the other; when Bill died at home in 1992 Annie, as promised, gently touched him and whispered, "Last tag."

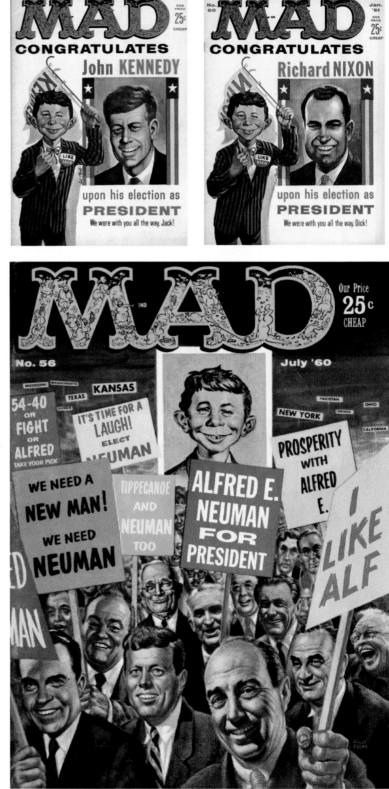

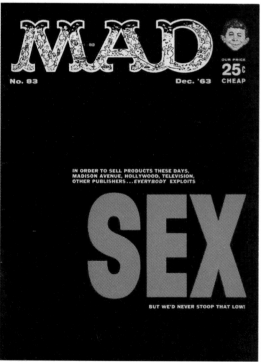

INSTANT PHOTOGRAPHY BY LESTER KRAUSS

Why we always look angry in these ad? I tell you why! We work hard – 12, maybe 14 hour a day – grow finest coffee tree – pick ripest bean – lift heavy sack – carry to boat – sweat and strain – and for what? So big company can grind it into lousy instant coffee because American housewife too lazy to brew real coffee, and American husband too spineless to object!
SUCKA INSTANT COFFEE... for "sucka" husband.

GENEROUS
FOOLS
PRODUCTS

"On our trip across the U.S.A. I posed Mama against interesting backgrounds like this, and got 11-by-14 blowups for detailed study!"

Nikita Khrushchev says: "It was <u>easy as borscht</u>

taking Kossacolor pictures like these!"

Russia's Beloved Premier uses Kossacolor Film ... and shows the NKVD boys how easy it is to take pictures of <u>interest</u>!

"It's natural for a tourist to carry a camera," chuckles Premier Nikita Khrushchev, "which made it *easy* for me to take wonderful pictures during my tour of the United States. And Kossacolor Film insured clear, sharp backgrounds for close scrutiny by our Intelligence Service. Yes, sir, Kossacolor made my trip to America *profitable!*"

"Here's Rada, my daughter, standing beside a secret atomic pile. Kossacolor gave me the picture. The pile gave Rada blood-poisoning!"

"I shot Alexei, my son-in-law, looking over Admiral Rickover's shoulder. I shot him again when we got home for covering the blueprints!"

"This is Julia, my other daughter. She moved when I took this picture, but the Radar Installation didn't!"

See Kossak's "What's My Party Line?" and "I've Got The Secrets"

EASTZONE KOSSAK COMPANY, Moscow 4, U. S. S. R.

Kossak
Trade Mark

FROM THE RUMMIE WALKER COLLECTION

"Crocked" by FRANK KELLY FREAS

Artist·Illustrator·Drunk

When we commissioned Frank Kelly Freas to paint his hobby for our ad campaign, we hoped he would come up with something as interesting as Harold Von Schmidt and Peter Helck and Robert Riggs had done before him. Unfortunately, it looks like Mr. Freas went a little astray after painting our whiskey bottle. Mainly, he killed the contents and ended up stewed to the gills.

Guess the laugh's really on us. We never figured Mr. Freas's hobby would turn out to be "drinking"!

RUMMIE WALKER
Took his first drink in 1820 still going strong

RUMMIE WALKER · BLACK LABEL · SCOTCH WHISKEY

WHAT SORT OF MAN READS MAD?

A young man with an open mind and a sharp sense of humor, the MAD reader has very little else to recommend him. He dresses atrociously, his tastes run to the ridiculous, and he's usually flat broke. If he does have any money, he spends it on idiotic things like the kookie car in the picture. (Incidentally, the young man beside the car isn't the MAD reader; the young man *underneath* the car is the MAD reader!) So actually, if you are an advertiser, it really wouldn't pay you to advertise in MAD. Facts: According to an obscure magazine survey, 97% of the 1,300,000 copies of MAD sold on newsstands each issue are purchased by clods. 87.3% of these clods have no visible means of support. And 79% wouldn't *believe* your advertising pitch anyway, because they've been thoroughly brainwashed by MAD articles and ad satires. So if you're looking for a magazine with a readership that seems to fall for the phony sophisticated soft sell, and has the money to do something about it, try PLAYBOY!

MAD ADVERTISING DEPARTMENT • Elevator Shaft #2 • 225 Lafayette Street, New York City , New York

LITHO IN U.S.A

You think you're alone on the highway. Now to test that premium gas you've been paying so much for. You push the pedal to the floor—and then you hear the siren. "Where's the *Fire, Chief?*" sneers the Trooper. And as he writes your ticket, you realize that having "the nearest thing to perfect gasoline" is pretty ridiculous when speed limits won't let you use it!

Trust your car will be stopped by the man who wears the star

MOE LAHR, D.D.S.
32 ABCESS PLACE PLYMOUTH, WASH

FOR DENTAL SERVICES RENDERED

July 8
1 Filling ——————— $1

July 15
1 Filling ——————— $1

July 22
1 Filling ——————— $1

July 29
Extraction ——————— $2

adds up to —— $5

PLEASE REMIT *IMMEDIATELY*

The best friend your dentist ever had

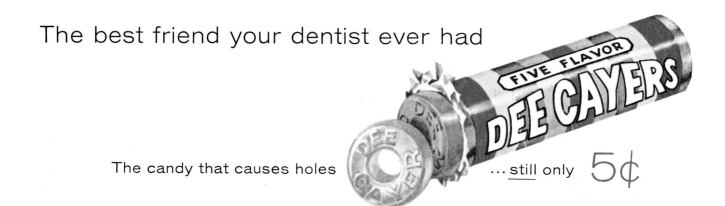

FIVE FLAVOR **DEE CAYERS**

The candy that causes holes

...still only 5¢

Fool-Aid

INSTANT
ANTIDOTE
FOR
ADULTS
FOOL
ENOUGH
TO BUY
SOFT
DRINKS
LITTLE
KIDS MAKE

There's always need for Fool-Aid. The hideous grin on the pitcher tells you it's indispensable. Warm weather brings out hordes of enterprising kids who set up soft drink stands in every neighborhood. The only trouble is: you can't be sure what the little monsters use to make the stuff. So be prepared! Always carry Fool-Aid — the instant antidote for poisons taken internally.

GENERAL FOOLS
PROTECTION

Is it true... blondes have more fun?

Just being a blonde is no guarantee, honey! Take our word for it! Because even if you do suffer thru 3 or 4 hours . . . stripping your hair of its old color with cream developer and protinator (which burns like hell), then washing the gook out, then towel-drying it, **then coloring your hair** with chemicals and peroxide, then rinsing, setting, combing it out, and starting all over again in a week — when the roots begin to show . . . Well, men will *still* get nauseous when they see you — if you happen to be ugly in the first place!

Even hairdressers will tell you an ugly blonde's best friend is **Lady Clinic** Plastic Surgeons

Newsweak

A **MAD** SATIRE COVER FOR CAMOUFLAGE PURPOSES

POSED BY OSCAR JORDAN, MEMBER A F T R A
PHOTOGRAPHY BY LESTER KRAUSS

"*This* We Bury First!"

—Nikita Khrushchev

YOU'LL GET A BANG OUT OF THIS ISSUE OF **MAD**

MEMO FROM **MAD**

THIS ALTERNATE BACK COVER ESPECIALLY DESIGNED FOR THOSE TOO ASHAMED TO BE SEEN WITH GARISH, SHOCKING FRONT COVER! NOW PEOPLE WILL THINK YOU ARE READING INTELLECTUAL "NEWS" MAGAZINE!

CRANKS A-MILLION DEPT.

When we were kids, we learned a simple and rather succinct phrase which pretty well summed up what Democracy was all about—mainly "The Majority Wins!" Unfortunately, the television industry doesn't seem to believe in this. Rather, they insist upon remaining at the mercy of so-called "Public Opinion" in the form of a few crank letters. Instead of fighting back, the networks prefer a more civilized way out, called "total surrender." To show how this sorry situation works out, we've prepared this behind-the-scenes study which demonstrates the power of the relative minority who write...

PROTEST LETTERS

ARTIST: BOB CLARKE   WRITER: SY REIT

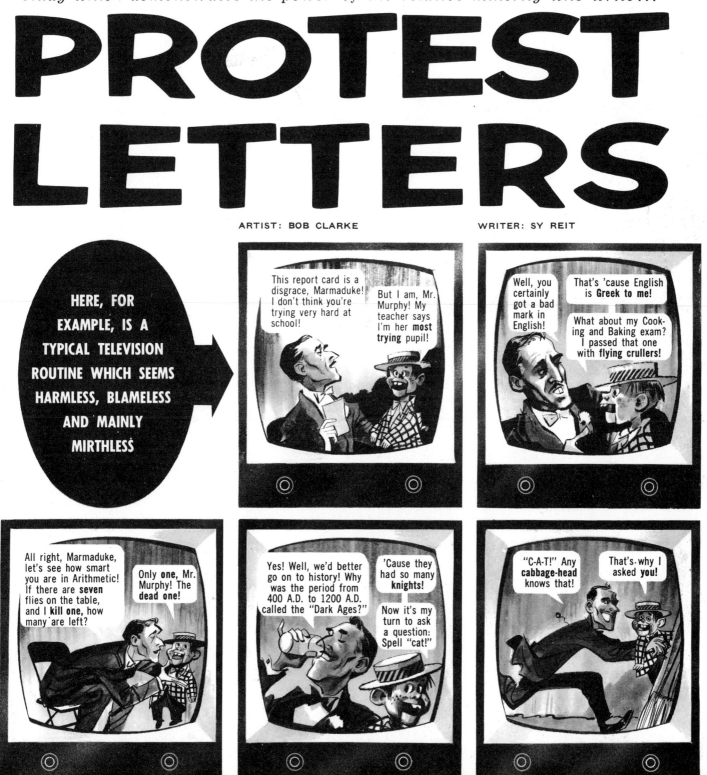

Dear Sirs,

I found your use of the name "Marmaduke" for the little boy in last night's show extremely offensive. I don't think there's anything funny about the name and I resent the implication that people with this name are usually stupid, or dummies, or something like that. Why don't you use a name like "Stanley," or "Horace," or "Melvin." Those are funny names!

yours truly,
Marmaduke Sternwallow III

Gentlemen,

As recording secretary of our local P.T.A., I must say I was shocked at the way you ridiculed education on last night's show! A poor report card is no laughing matter! How can we instill respect for learning in our children when they are exposed to shows like yours, lampooning our educational system?

—Angry Mother

Gentlemen—

Last night you showed Marmaduke wearing a straw hat, indoors! How can we teach our kids good manners when you set such a bad example for them?

Television is a vital force in today's community. When are you people going to wake up to your responsibilities?

—Despairing Father

Fearless, Inc.

COVERS THE COUNTRY

May 25th, 1959

Gentlemen:

Last night you showed Marmaduke wearing a straw hat. Don't you realize that this sort of thing can ruin the felt hat industry?

Television is a vital force in today's community. When are you people going to wake up to your responsibilities?

Cordially,

Kendall Fosdick

President,
Fearless Felt Hat M'f'g Co.

GREEK CONSULATE
Washington, D. C.

Dear Ιδιαιτέρως: —

'Εφήμερίδες τῆς Δυτικῆς Εὐρωπς υπογραμμιξουν σήμερον, ότι ἡ Σοβιετική εκδοχὴ τῆς ἐν Μόσχα λογομαχιὰς '' —English is Greek to me!'' μεταξύ τοῦ Αντιπροέδρου τῶν morons! 'Ηνωμένων Πολιτειῶν καὶ του πρωθυπυρ dumbkopfs! Δὲν να διστασω να επαναρχίσω τον αγῶνα big law-suit!

Sincerely yours,

Herman Hellespont

Consul General

Dear Sirs,

Since your program is watched by millions of youngsters all over the country, the use of suggestive material is uncalled for and unforgivable.

Your ventriloquist's reference to so many knights, (sic nights) during the dark ages is an obvious and deliberate attempt to inject sex into a family show.

Is a high Trendex rating excuse enough to throw good taste to the winds? If this practice continues, I will forbid my children to watch your program! and my grandchildren too!

Shocked Parent

DEAR MARMADUKE AND MR MURPHY—

YOUR SHOW STINKS. OKAY MAYBE FOR A THREE OR FOUR YEAR OLD BUT NOT FOR BIG KIDZ LIKE ME IM FIVE

SINSERELY YOURS
JIMMY AXOLOTL

May 25, 1959

Dear Sirs

I'm getting sick and tired of the way you people always make cats the butt of your jokes. Why did the man have to spell CAT? why not DOG or CHIPMUNK or AARDVAARK?

Speaking for thousands of cat lovers, this sort of treatment must stop! I am throwing away my TV set.

disgustedly
Elvira Tuttle

Gentlemen:

Despite the fact that we work long hours, and are extremely underpaid, teachers here in America are still maligned and insulted at every turn.

Your show last night gave the impression that all we do is joke and kid around with our pupils.

You would have done better to show how difficult our job is, trying to teach children in overcrowded classrooms with limited facilities.

The future of America lies with our young people, and the future of our young people lies with their teachers.

Our responsibilities are great! and so are yours! Let's have no more of this!

—Indignant Teacher

—May 25, 1959

Dear Sir:—

I am a teen-ager. I think your show was a deliberate slap at teen-agers. Why does everyone pick on teen-agers?

All that stuff about school and report cards, and stuff. What's funny about school and report cards?

You probably hate rock and roll, too! and Fabian. Everybody is against us teenagers!

Wait till we take over!

—M.B.

What have you guys got against the Cooks and Bakers Union, anyway? What are you—a bunch of anti-labor smart alecs?

paid up member of Local 842

Gentlemen:

Things have come to a shocking state in this great big grand and glorious country of ours when television comedians stoop so low as to make fun of our great big grand and glorious flag.

I am referring to last night's show in which your ventriloquist called our flying colors: "flying crullers"!

Have you checked this commies past affiliations?

—Proud American

AMERICAN SOCIETY FOR THE PREVENTION OF CRUELTY TO ANIMALS

May 25th, 1959

Dear Sirs:—

On behalf of our membership, I hereby protest your reference in last night's television program to the killing of flies. How long, sirs, must this wanton disregard for insect life continue? Will the senseless slaughter never cease? The fly, I admit, is not without its faults—but let us try to remember that it is still one of Nature's creatures. If more of us tried to see things from the fly's point of view, what a happier, kindlier place our world would be. This applies to the entire genus "Diptera," including gnats, fleas and mosquitos.

Respectfully,
RODNEY MUDGE
Secretary

S.P.H.A.

Society for the Preservation of Historic Accuracy

May 25th, 1959

Dear Sirs:—

Contrary to the statement on your television program, the Dark Ages did not extend from 400 A.D. to 1200 A.D. Scholars generally agree that the Dark (or Middle) Ages may be said to commence with the fall of the Western Roman Empire, in 476, and terminate with the discovery of America by Columbus in 1492. No doubt you will be anxious to correct this grievous error immediately.

We suggest a complete and frank statement by the President of your Company, to be made on a combined international, multi-channel network. Hoping we will not be compelled to take further steps, I am,

Sincerely,

J. Finchley Doob
Associate Director

Protective Association
National Cabbage Growers

Dear Sirs: 25 May, 1959

The use of the phrase "cabbage-head" is an uncalled-for slur. For your information, the cabbage has served long and well in building healthy bodies and helping to keep our nation strong. It is regrettable that you must look for so-called "laughs" at the expense of an innocent and harmless vegetable. Our organization feels that a retraction is in order.

Very truly yours,

Gertrude Vetch,
Director

gv:svr

Gentlemen—

The dummy on your TV show looks exactly like my daughter, Henrietta. Unless you apologize publicly I will turn this matter over to my lawyers.

sincerely,
Albert Furd

SO, AFTER A WHILE, WHEN THE SHOW WAS DUE FOR A RE-RUN, THE NETWORK DECIDED TO PLAY IT SAFE

THEY CUT OUT EVERYTHING THEY KNEW TO BE OF A CONTROVERSIAL NATURE, AND RAN WHAT THEY HAD LEFT

AND IT WORKED FINE, BECAUSE ONLY ONE LETTER OF PROTEST TURNED UP THE FOLLOWING DAY

NBC
30 Rockefeller Plaza
New York 20, N. Y.

August 24, 1959

Dear Murphy and Marmaduke:-

As per our option clause (Para. 71, Lines 181-3), your contract with this network is hereby cancelled.

The Trendex rating on last night's show was terrible. It is obvious that your popularity has waned. Something seemed to be lacking in your performance. You just weren't your "old selves" on last night's show. Therefore, we feel that the only solution is to drop your program.

Sincerely yours,

Robert Sarnoff
President

Murph, I don't know what to say! I simply can't understand what happened. Certainly, it's no fault of ours here at the network. All I can say is, oh well—that's show biz!

Bob

"Just relax and tell me everything that comes into your mind!"

And now, Don Martin tells us a souped-up tale of his experience

In a "GREASY SPOON" Diner

"The MAD Horror Primer" (Issue #49) received such a GREAT response from our readers (i.e. *"A GREAT disappointment!"*—B.F., Phila., Pa.; *"It would be GREAT if you discontinued this type feature!"*—L.D., Dallas, Tex.; *"Articles like that GRATE on my nerves!"*—F.H., Fresno, Calif.) that we've decided to present another primer. This one is for the benefit of any children under seven (in other words, ALL of our readers) who may possibly be interested in working in the advertising field when they grow up.

THE MAD MADISON AVENUE PRIMER

ARTIST: WALLACE WOOD   WRITER: LARRY SIEGEL

MY FIRST READER
(EDUCATION-WISE)
Rock-Bottom Slants for Little Group-Noodlers

By Batton, Barton, Durstine & Cowznofsky

Lesson 3

See the pretty street.
It is called "Madison Avenue".
All the ad-men work here.
They write "Winston tastes good . . ." here.
Write, write, write.
They write "Mr. Clean, Mr. Clean . . ." here.
Write, write, write.
Don't you wish YOU could write like that?
You can.
You're almost *seven* now.

Lesson 4

See the nice advertising agency.
400 nice people work here.
Let us count the 400 nice people.
Count, count, count.
Hmmm! 300 nice people are missing.
The nice advertising agency must have
    lost another nice $4-million account.
Dear, dear, dear.
Where are the 300 nice people now?
At the nice Unemployment Insurance office.
Sign, sign, sign.
Isn't job security nice on Madison Avenue?

Lesson 1

See the man.
He does advertising work.
He is called an "ad-man".
See his funny tight suit.
See his funny haircut.
Hear his funny stomach churn.
Churn, churn, churn.
The ad-man has a funny ulcer.
Most ad-men have funny ulcers.
But, then, some ad-men are lucky.
They do *not* have funny ulcers.
They have funny high blood pressure.

Lesson 2

See the ad-man run.
Run, ad-man, run.
The ad-man must catch the 8:02.
All ad-men must catch the 8:02.
It is a fast commuter train.
It is never more than two hours late.
And it has a club car.
"All aboard!" says the conductor.
"Chug, chug!" says the train.
"Gulp, gulp!" says the ad-man.
Wouldn't *you* like Bourbon for breakfast, too?

Lesson 5

See the kindly old man.
He is the President of the agency.
He has fired 132 people today.
And it isn't even lunch time yet.
Fire, fire, fire.
See the fine young man with him.
He will not be fired, today.
He is a fine ad-man.
He is a fine Vice-President of the agency.
He is a fine son of the President of the agency.

Lesson 6

See the Account Executive.
His accounts are Puffo Cigarettes,
    Bubble Soap, and Flaky Cereal.
The agency loves and trusts him.
Kiss, kiss, kiss.
Trust, trust, trust.
Next week he will resign.
He will form his own agency.
He will have three accounts in his agency.
They will be Puffo Cigarettes,
    Bubble Soap, and Flaky Cereal.
Bounce, bounce, bounce.
That's the way the ball bounces on Madison Avenue.

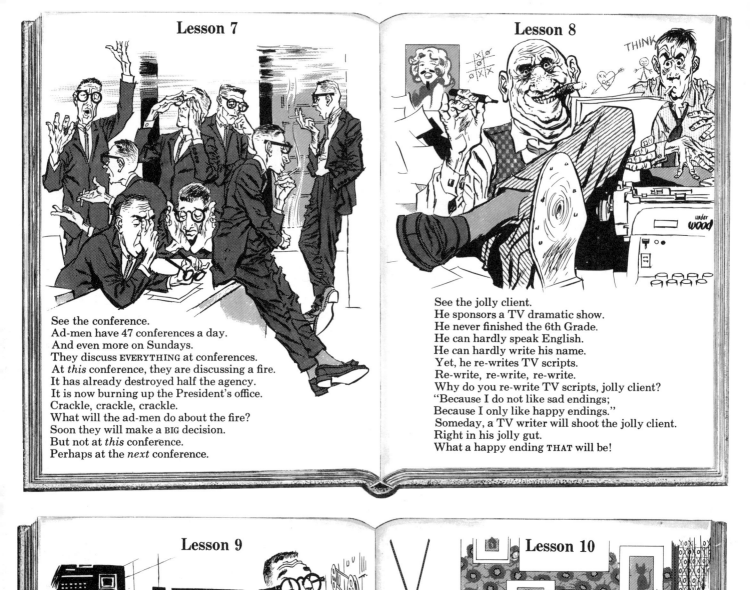

Lesson 7

See the conference.
Ad-men have 47 conferences a day.
And even more on Sundays.
They discuss EVERYTHING at conferences.
At *this* conference, they are discussing a fire.
It has already destroyed half the agency.
It is now burning up the President's office.
Crackle, crackle, crackle.
What will the ad-men do about the fire?
Soon they will make a BIG decision.
But not at *this* conference.
Perhaps at the *next* conference.

Lesson 8

See the jolly client.
He sponsors a TV dramatic show.
He never finished the 6th Grade.
He can hardly speak English.
He can hardly write his name.
Yet, he re-writes TV scripts.
Re-write, re-write, re-write.
Why do you re-write TV scripts, jolly client?
"Because I do not like sad endings;
Because I only like happy endings."
Someday, a TV writer will shoot the jolly client.
Right in his jolly gut.
What a happy ending THAT will be!

Lesson 9

See the man rate a TV show.
See how he arrives at a scientific rating.
First he makes 10 phone calls.
Then he puts 10 numbers in his hat.
Then he closes his eyes tight.
Then he picks the scientific rating out of his hat.
Oh-oh! This TV show's rating is $6\frac{3}{8}$.
Ho-ho! He has made a scientific mistake.
He has picked out his scientific *hat size*.
But it is too late.
It was such a nice TV show, too.
It cost three million dollars, too.
It might have remained on the air, too.
If the man had a bigger head.

Lesson 10

See the amazing average clod.
He is the Eighth Wonder of the World.
He has a 40-year-old body and a 10-year-old mind.
According to Madison Avenue.
So they write TV commercials especially for him.
And they write magazine ads especially for him.
If this keeps up, the amazing average clod will
    become even more amazing.
He will no longer have a 40-year-old body and a
    10-year-old mind.
He will have a 40-year-old body and a
    FIVE-year-old mind.

There seems to be a rash of new musicals slated for Broadway based on the "Madison Avenue" theme. Since one of the most successful musicals ever to hit Broadway was "My Fair Lady," based on the book by George Bernard Shaw, we figure it won't be long before we'll be seeing a hit "Madison Avenue" musical along the same lines and called . . .

My Fair Ad-Man

BASED ON THE BOOK "YOU'RE A PIG, MALLION" BY GEORGE BERNARD SCHWARTZ

ARTIST: MORT DRUCKER

WRITER: NICK MEGLIN

We know about "Russian Roulette" . . . the game where you have a six-shooter with one bullet and you keep pulling the trigger until somebody loses by getting killed. And we know about "Magazine Roulette" . . . the game where you have six magazines and you keep choosing one until somebody loses by picking MAD. But the most vicious game we know is the one that millions of Americans play every

COMMERCIAL

day. That's the game where you have six TV channels and you keep turning to each, trying to find some entertainment. The game starts when it's time for the commercial. Mainly, when you decide to switch it off. Because the TV networks are wise to this sneaky maneuver, and they've all scheduled their ads to come on at the same time. Here, then, is what it's like . . . when you're playing . . .

ROULETTE

WRITER: GARY BELKIN

**CHAMPS-ELYSEES—Floyd Patterson and Ingemar Johansson are lazy.

° ° LA PLUME DE MA TANTE—There's a plum in my tent.

S'matter, can't you Dial?!

No, this isn't Irving! What number do you want? Well, that's your

trouble, idiot! You got the wrong number! This is AT-7...not AT-6!

Why don't you learn how to Dial? People who like people Dial correctly!

Y'know, you dragged me out of a shower! Well,what's so funny about that?

Listen, do me a favor! After you learn how to Dial . . . drop dead!

PHOTO BY LESTER KRAUSS

Aren't
you glad
you Dial
correctly?

(Don't you wish everybody did?)

We do, because every time anybody's
dragged out of a shower to answer a
wrong number, he stops using up soap!

Send
for
this
free
book
today

HOW TO
dial
correctly
Courtesy of LUX Soap

Antonio Prohias is a famous Cuban artist whose anti-Castro cartoons have appeared in such publications as Bohemia (largest circulation of any Spanish language magazine), the daily *Prensa Libre* (Free Press) *El Mundo,* and the Sunday *Oveja Negra* (Black Sheep). He has won the "Juan Gualberto Gomez" award (the equivalent of our Cartoon Society's "Ruben") six times. On May 1st, three days before Castro henchmen took over what remained of Cuba's free press, Prohias fled to N.Y. stone broke. Once here, he came directly to MAD. Among the things he showed us was this captivating cartoon-sequence of friendly rivalry called

Scenes We'd Like to See

The Doctor's Pronouncement.

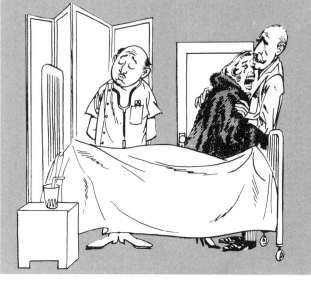

WRITER: AL JAFFEE

ARTIST: MORT DRUCKER

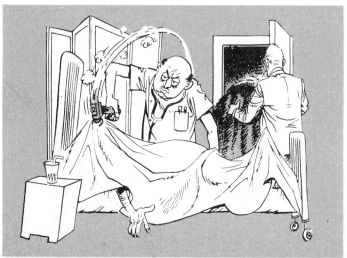

**A Play about Pavlov's Experiments with Dogs called "Bell, Bark and Kennel"

Now that Albert Einstein has gone to his Reward, and Charles Van Doren was caught accepting his, probably the most popular intelligent American today is television's canine star, Lizzie. Every week, millions of kids watch with awe as this fantastic Collie performs unbelievable feats of brilliance. And so, in fairness to all these gullible youngsters, we here at MAD now present the real truth about...

TV'S WONDER DOG
LIZZIE

ARTIST: MORT DRUCKER   WRITER: LARRY SIEGEL

**ET CETERA—He chewed up the scenery.

We are often asked what MAD'S maddest artist, Don Martin, really looks like — and if it's true that he resembles the characters he draws. Well, the answer is: No, he does not look like the people in his cartoons! Actually, due to his physical appearance, Don never planned on becoming an artist. He had much higher hopes — but his first offering of the issue shows you what happened to

A Young Man's AMBITION

**A Play about a Bleached Blonde called "Dark At The Base Of The Hairs"

DADDY-O KNOWS BEST DEPT.

Much has been written about the teenager of today—but in every article we've seen, one important fact has been overlooked or ignored: namely, that the teenager of today is the parent of to-morrow! Yes, frightening as it may seem, we cannot escape the fact that the rebellious adolescent of the present will someday become the mother-symbol and father-image for the rebellious adolescent of the future. So with this horrible thought in mind, MAD presents an article which sneaks a peek into the future for a glimpse of what it will be like when today's teenagers become . . .

TOMORROW'S PARENTS

ARTIST: WALLACE WOOD   WRITER: GARY BELKIN

By the 1970's, today's young people will have found the answer to their respective teenage prayers, and many of them will have gotten married and become parents. As all parents do, they will name their children after their own personal idols. The most popular names for boys in 1970 will be Fabian, Frankie, Frankenstein, Bobby, Darin and Elvis. The most popular names for girls in 1970 will be Sandra, Tuesday, Wednesday, Annette, Funicello and Elvis.

Here are two typical parents of 1975 — Fred and Ginger (named after their own parent's idols) Typical — proudly posing behind their two children: five-year-old Tuesday Sandra Typical, and six-year-old Kingston Trio Typical.

When Tuesday and Kingston reach their teens, they've got all the things Fred and Ginger's parents refused to give them: their own rooms, their own phones, monogrammed bongos, subscriptions to MAD, and a fifth-rate education.

Yet, despite all these advantages, Fred and Ginger sense that their children are not turning out "right." Tuesday and Kingston keep their rooms neat and clean, never leave clothes lying around, read books, drink milk, watch only Educational TV, hate Rock 'n Roll, don't go steady (even though both are well past 12), and actually enjoy school.

Sincerely worried about the strange behavior of their two teenage children, Fred and Ginger seek professional help. Reluctantly, they discuss the problem with a psychiatrist:

Temporarily relieved, Fred and Ginger resume their normal lives, hoping for the day when their children's rebellious phase will pass. But one day, that hope is shattered . . .

Kingston's remarks are prophetic. In years to come, Fred and Ginger will forgive and accept their children for what they are. However, having failed as doting parents, they will achieve astonishing success as doting grandparents. Because, just as their own children rebelled against them, their grandchildren will rebel against their own parents.

Everybody gets old! Everybody, that is, except most comic strip characters! These jokers have the uncanny ability to remain the same dull age year after year, getting into the same dull situations. So MAD's gonna break the monotony . . . bearing in mind that if these comic strip characters were to age, one good aspect would be that they'd soon die off and we wouldn't have to suffer through them any more. Anyway, let's take away their fountains of youth, and see what the future would be like . . .

SUPERMAN

IF
DICK TRACY
COMIC STRIP CHARACTERS WERE AS OLD AS THEIR STRIPS

POPEYE

ARTIST: WALLACE WOOD   WRITER: EARLE DOUD

LI'L ABNER

MANDRAKE THE MAGICIAN

TARZAN

HENRY

CALL AND SOON

©Ming Features Dynasty ink.

7-11

DENNIS THE MENACE

"As Chief U.S. Delegate to the United Nations, I would like to report that I have, through protracted discussion and extended mediation, accomplished the following: I have solved the Vietnam crisis ... I have straightened out the Berlin situation ... I have come up with a mutually acceptable disarmament plan ... and I've put chewing gum on all your seats!"

VENGEANCE

BY ANTONIO PROHIAS

Gilbert and Sullivan are famous for their operettas, and will long be remembered for their clever and light-hearted satire. MAD, on the other hand is notorious for its articles, and will hardly be remembered for its idiotic and heavy-handed satire. So, in a desperate effort to alter its corporate image, the clod-staff of

MAD MAGAZINE

(With apologies to Gilbert and Sullivan)

PRESENTS

A DAY WITH J-F-K

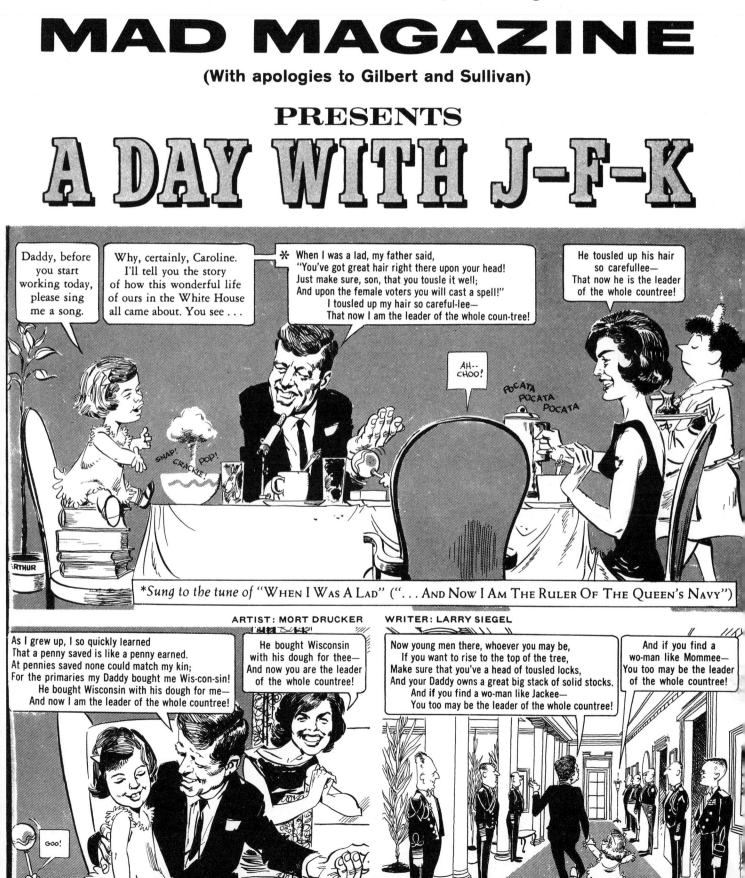

Does this ad look blurred to you?

It should look blurred to you. Mainly because it really is blurred. We photographed it out of focus on purpose, and we're printing it exactly like this in millions of magazines all over the country.

Why are we doing this? So you'll strain your eyes to read it, that's why!

We're also running ads with blurred pictures—so you'll strain your eyes on them, too!

We figure if you strain your eyes bad enough on all our ads, you'll end up needing glasses. Pretty sneaky, eh?

Well, it was the best way we could think of to get you into our offices and shops so we could take you for plenty by overcharging for lenses and frames and eye-drops and like that. We, being all the greedy Optometrists & Oculists in the Better Vision Business Assoc.

Several years ago, a Magazine Editor (who was probably separated from his wife) coined the word, "togetherness." And it took the country by storm. We were bombarded with messages of "togetherness" by magazines, newspapers, skywriting, and even deodorant commercials. Now, thanks to television, the ultimate in "togetherness" has been achieved . . . The Family Western. Gone are the gunfights and the killing and the brutality. Instead, we're getting love and romance and even compatible color—in . . .

BANANAZ
The "Family Togetherness" Western

ARTIST: MORT DRUCKER

WRITERS: EARLE DOUD

Practically everybody has seen "West Side Story"— which is about a couple of tough gangs on New York's West Side. Well, we think the producers of this show really missed the boat. Like, they went to the wrong side. If they thought the gangs on the West Side were tough, they should have taken a look at those two rival gangs on the East Side — mainly those two rival gangs at the U.N.! Because if they had, they might have come up with a musical called:

EAST SIDE STORY

ARTIST: MORT DRUCKER
WRITER: FRANK JACOBS

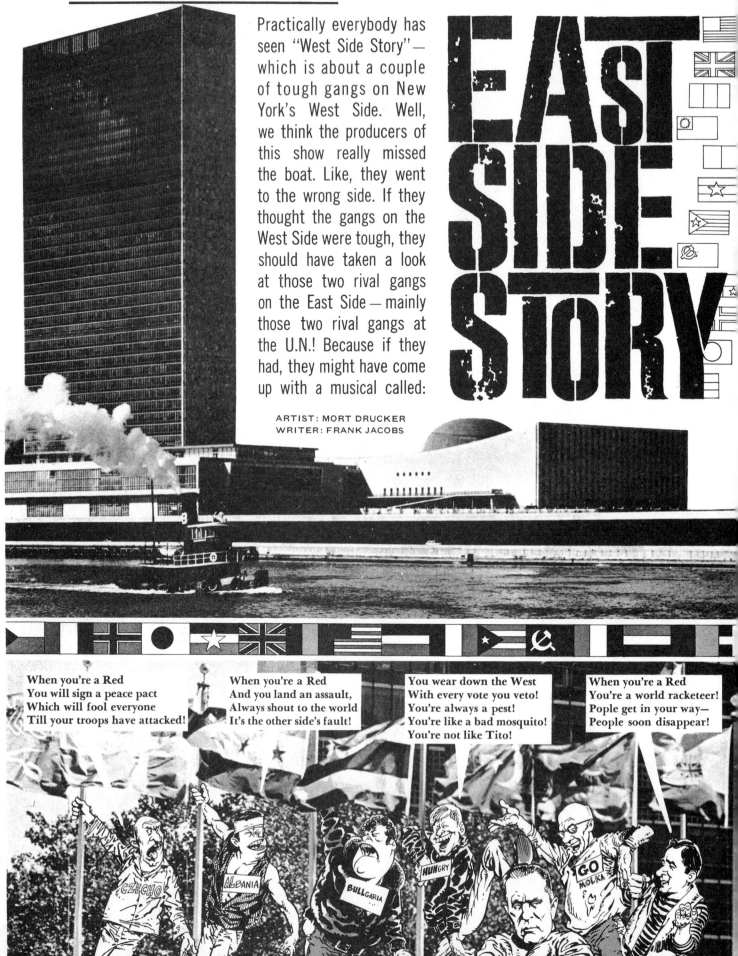

When you're a Red
You will sign a peace pact
Which will fool everyone
Till your troops have attacked!

When you're a Red
And you land an assault,
Always shout to the world
It's the other side's fault!

You wear down the West
With every vote you veto!
You're always a pest!
You're like a bad mosquito!
You're not like Tito!

When you're a Red
You're a world racketeer!
Pople get in your way—
People soon disappear!

RUSSIAN "RUSSIAN ROULETTE"

ARTIST & WRITER: SERGIO ARAGONES

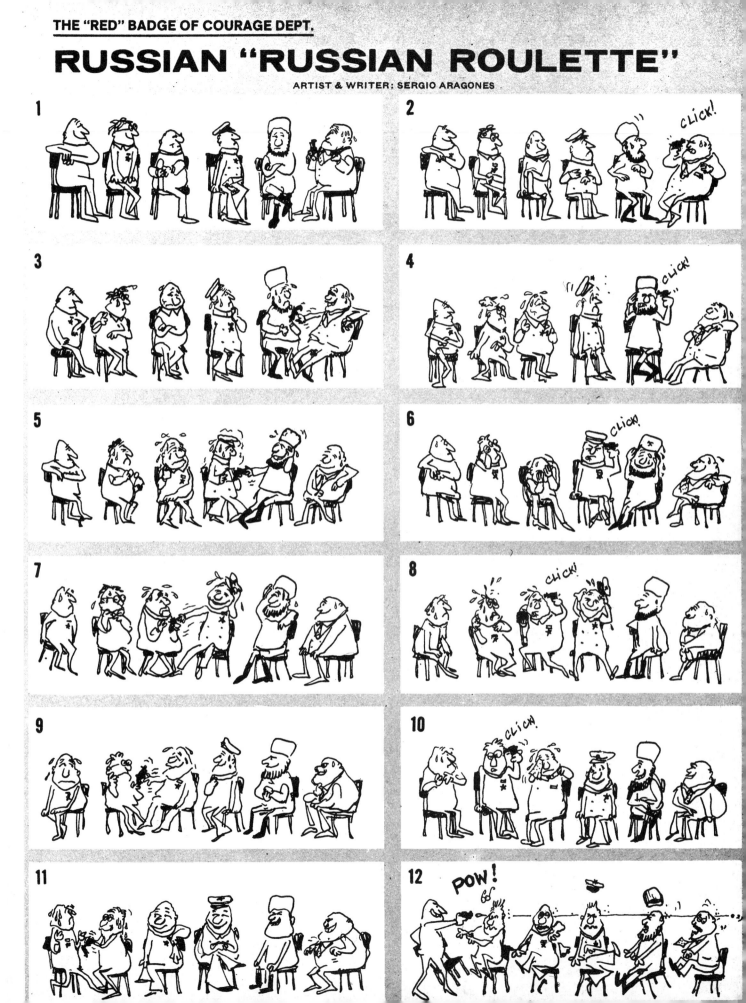

THEY DREW WHAT THEY WANTED DEPT.

We at MAD feel that the designs of today's Christmas toys reflect our warped adult sense of values. We at MAD also feel that the success of today's Christmas toys exposes our basic insecurity as parents trying to buy the love of our children with material things. But mainly, we at MAD feel too cheap to spend that money on our kids! So here is our idea: Instead of nuclear physicists designing complicated costly toys, why not let kids design them? Children's drawings show simple, beautiful, joyous viewpoints that no grown-up can hope to capture. Here, then, is what we would be seeing . . .

IF KIDS
THEIR O

STORY AND MODELS BY AL JAFFEE

Dolls have become so complicated and realistic today, they're almost human. But little girls don't want human dolls. If you don't believe it, watch how little girls torture baby brothers or sisters. We interrupted little Karen Shmutz while she was sticking her finger down her baby brother's throat, and asked her to design this doll.

DESIGNED OWN XMAS TOYS

PHOTOS BY LESTER KRAUSS

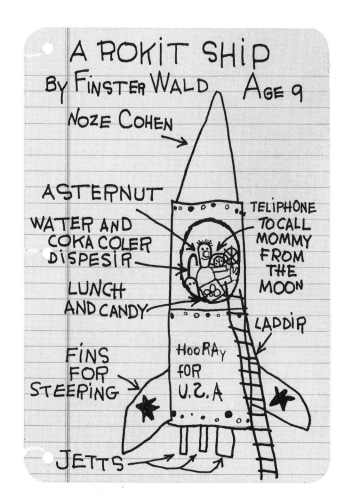

A ROKIT SHIP
BY FINSTER WALD   AGE 9

NOZE COHEN

ASTERNUT

TELIPHONE TO CALL MOMMY FROM THE MOON

WATER AND COKA COLER DISPESIR

LUNCH AND CANDY

LADDIR

FINS FOR STEERING

HOORAY FOR U.Z.A

JETTS

Nine year old Finster Wald's design for a rocket ship seems far more interesting to us than the realistic ones turned out by areo-space scientists working for toy companies. And it probably works as well as the ones these guys designed for the U.S. space effort before they left to go to work for the toy companies.

THE SUPERCHIF WAGIN
BY SHELDON SHNOOK AGE 7½

HANDEL

DRVRS SEET

PASSINGER SEETS

SUPER CHIF

WEELS (4)

Notice the brilliant new concepts that 7-and-one-half year old Sheldon Shnook's wagon introduces to the toymaker's art . . . brilliant new concepts like crooked sides . . . wheels that won't turn . . . and perspectives that haven't even been discovered yet! But Sheldon's wagon has one thing that no one can take away from it: its inner beauty . . . namely, its low price!

A
~~Jet~~ ~~An~~
Airplane

by Charles E. Gidroole
Age 10 years and
2 munths

by Charles E. Gidrool

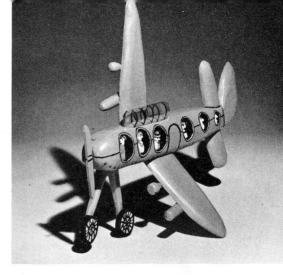

Charlie misses nothing when he sees a jet airplane. Of course, he misses plenty when he draws one . . . but we think it's grand anyway. His attention to detail is enchanting. It's also a bit cockeyed, but that's okay because we're hoping some forward-looking toy company will manufacture Charlie's plane and he'll make enough money on royalties to afford the glasses he needs.

As Americans, one of our most admirable traits is the ability we have to laugh at ourselves and make light of serious matters. Even Cape Canaveral couldn't escape the humorous onslaughts directed its way by such comics

A MAD LOOK AT THE

s Nichols and May ("But, Mother—I was sending up Vanguard!"), Bill Dana
"I'm gonna cry a lot!"), Charlie Manna ("I'm not goin' without my crayons!"),
tc. And so, in answer to many requests that we add our observations, here's

U.S. SPACE EFFORT

ARTIST & WRITER: SERGIO ARAGONES

THE PARTING SHOT

ARTIST: JOE ORLANDO

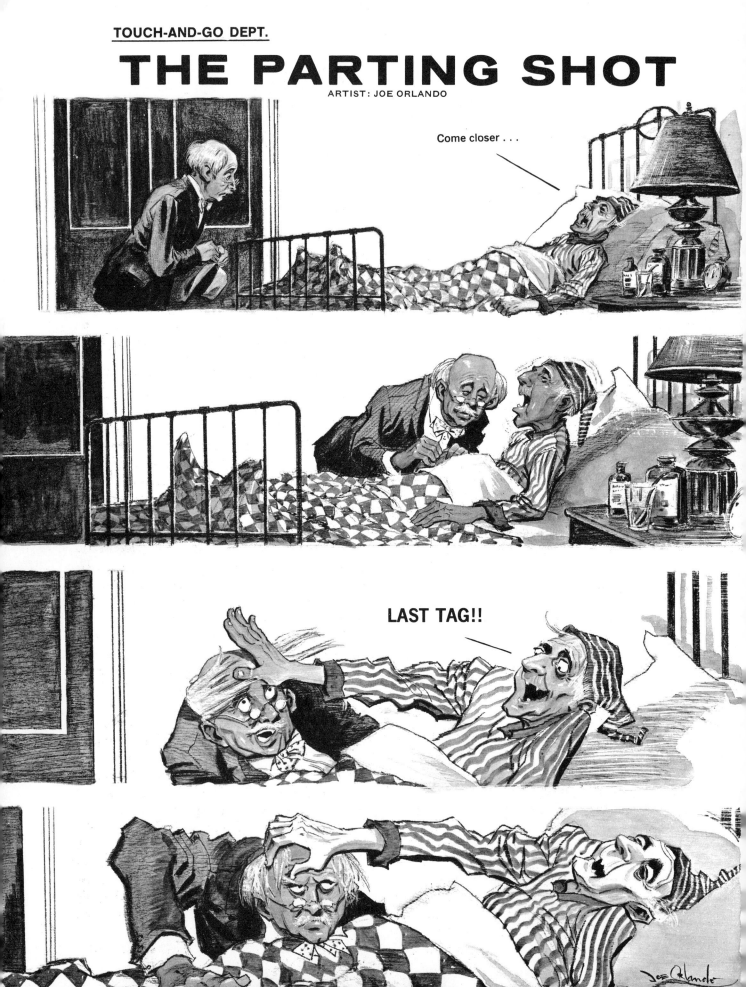

Early 1964: The nation is still reeling from the November 22, 1963, assassination of President John F. Kennedy. On February 9th a musical group from Liverpool, England, with a new sound and shockingly long hair appears on the *Ed Sullivan Show* to an audience of seventy million viewers; Beatlemania sweeps the country. Ford Motors introduces in April a sporty new model car that becomes an instant classic: the Mustang, priced at $2,368. And "the usual gang of idiots" stumbles onward.

The Norman Mingo cover of issue #89 (September 1964) is a takeoff on the plastic model kit/monster craze of the early to mid-sixties. Many of the classic movie monsters were then available in kit form from Aurora (Frankenstein's Monster, The Wolfman, Dracula, The Mummy, et cetera), under license from Universal. Alfred had a model kit of his own (also made by Aurora, priced at the time at $1.49), which made for an amusing reverse twist cover idea. Universal, who owned the rights to the famous bolt-necked image of the Frankenstein monster, was not amused and threatened legal action. However, like many such legal threats against the magazine, no actual suit was pursued.

Adorning the cover of issue #93 (March 1965) was the "MAD POIUYT," which was an optical illusion MAD bought from a contributor who claimed it was original. The readers soon pointed out, to the staff's embarrassment, that the image had appeared in many different publications over the previous year. The name "POIUYT," of course, is the last six letters of the second row of a typewriter, in reverse.

Issue #94's cover (April 1965) was inspired by Bill Gaines's love of big things in general, and of King Kong in particular. Around the same time, Sergio Aragonés made a life-size papier-mâché head of King Kong to fit into the window in Gaines's office; it still resides in the MAD office today. Sprinkled around the magazine during this period (and a year or so before) were various MAD icons: the "MAD Zeppelin," Arthur the avocado plant, and a scrawny, long-necked bird who also seemed to have no particular significance.

The "painting the road" cover of issue #96 (July 1965) is quintessentially MAD: absurd, surreal, and funny. Note the low-flying "MAD Zeppelin" just above the horizon. The 100th issue of the magazine (January 1966) was celebrated in typical self-deprecating fashion: "Big Deal!"

In January 1964 the Federal Trade Commission proposed plans to require warning labels on cigarette packs and to ban cigarette advertisements featuring endorsements by athletes. MAD had long held an anti-smoking stance, and with the evidence of the health risks mounting, the magazine embarked on a relentless series of parodies of cigarette advertisements. One such parody, "Likely Strife," appears in this section. MAD staffers again play the parts: The ad features De Fuccio, Meglin, and Putnam. Also appearing: Lenny Brenner in the "Concertina" ad and Bill Gaines as "Arnold Finster" in the "Bilked Telephone System" ad.

The "Beautiful Hair—Blecch" parody is one of the all-time classic ad parodies ever to appear in MAD. The piece appeared on the back cover of issue #90 (October 1964, but on the newsstands in August). Although tame by today's standards, in 1964 Beatle haircuts were the subject of great debate, not to mention parental indignation. Frank Frazetta did the gorgeous rendering of the doe-eyed Ringo Starr. Frazetta had done some work on Gaines's EC comics, and by the mid-sixties had become a very successful commercial artist, doing paintings for book covers, record jackets, and movie posters. Today, Frank Frazetta is considered the premier fantasy illustrator, and his works have sold in the six-figure range. Frazetta's only other piece for MAD, "Early One Morning in the Jungle" (issue #106, October 1966), appears in this section as well. The original artwork for "Early One Morning in the Jungle" was auctioned by Christie's in December 1992 for an amazing $30,800.

The "MAD's Great Moments in Advertising— Hertz" is a parody of a popular and long-running series of television ads for Hertz Car Rentals. The spot used "flying" people to show how fast Hertz could get travelers in their cars and on their way. The MAD twist: what if the top were left up? A similar idea was used as a running gag in the farcical film *Good Neighbor Sam* (1964), which starred Jack Lemmon as a high-strung ad man. The other "Great Moments in Advertising" parody appearing here juxtaposes two different advertising characters: the Jolly Green Giant and the Action detergent Genie, who usually popped out of the washer.

Al Jaffee's "Fold-Ins" have been one of MAD's

most popular features for more than thirty years. The first-ever "MAD Fold-In" (MAD #86, April 1964) appears in this section. The early "Fold-Ins" were printed in black and white, since MAD didn't begin running full color on the inside covers until the middle of 1968. Another Jaffee favorite, "Snappy Answers to Stupid Questions," spawned a long series of paperback books. The first "Snappy Answers" is presented here, from MAD #98 (October 1965).

"The Phewgitive" is MAD's send-up of *The Fugitive*, the popular television drama that ran from 1963 to 1967. The series starred David Janssen as Dr. Richard Kimble, who was on a quest for his wife's killer, the elusive "one-armed man." The final episode of the series, where Kimble finally catches up with the "one-armed man," had one of the largest viewing audiences in television history.

"A Celebrity's Wallet: Ringo Starr" is a very funny take on the then brand-new Beatles phenomenon. Like Sinatra in the forties and Elvis in the fifties, the Beatles were considered by their detractors to be just a very bright flash in the pan, little more than a fabulously successful combination of hype, hairstyle, and luck. Especially noteworthy in this piece is the "letter" from Moe of the Three Stooges and the inclusion of MAD's own "Blecch" parody ad.

Dave Berg's "The Lighter Side of . . ." is another long-running and well-loved feature. The piece in this section looks at "Teenage Parties." As usual, Berg handles his subject with a gentle and affectionate humor.

The "43-Man Squamish" article, by George Woodbridge and Tom Koch, developed a life of its own beyond the pages of MAD. Introduced as a MAD alternative to collegiate sports like football and basketball, the game's utterly indecipherable rules and the large number of players required made it impossible to play. In spite of this, "43-Man Squamish" was all the rage for a time on college campuses, with numerous "Squamish" teams being formed. How the teams managed to play the game is a mystery, but perhaps the impossibly absurd nature of the game was the very thing that accounted for its popularity.

"The Man from A.U.N.T.I.E." sends up *The Man from U.N.C.L.E.*, which was the first TV series inspired by James Bond–style secret agents. The series opening featured agents Solo and Kuryakin entering the tailor shop that served as the "front" to the secret U.N.C.L.E. headquarters. Writer Arnie Kogen's MAD version begins with the agents, Polo and Nutcrackin, entering through the wrong tailor shop.

Jack Davis, one of America's most versatile and brilliant cartoonists, was one of the original MAD artists. Davis worked on Harvey Kurtzman's MAD as far back as the first issue and left with Kurtzman to work on Hugh Hefner's ill-fated and short-lived *Trump* magazine. After almost ten years of every kind of freelance work imaginable (including work on several inferior MAD imitations), Davis rejoined "the usual gang of idiots." "Horror Movie Scenes We'd Like to See" (MAD #99, December 1965) is the first piece Davis illustrated upon his return, done in his trademark "crosshatched" style. "Horror Movie Scenes" writer Don Edwing will be familiar to current MAD readers as artist/writer "Duck" Edwing.

In 1966 a show that was the very essence of the word "camp" appeared on TV screens. The show was called *Batman*, and it launched an intense but relatively short-lived "Bat-craze." Starring Adam West as Batman, the series was based on the popular DC comic book super hero but done with tongue firmly in cheek. Filmed with off-kilter camera angles, bright primary colors, comic book–style sound effects ("BIFF!," "POW!!," "BANG!!!"), and campy dialogue like "Holy Batcave, Batman!," the show became an overnight sensation. However entertaining and successful *Batman* was, though, it unfortunately set the notion of comic books as adult entertainment back by at least twenty years. MAD's spin on the program focused on "Sparrow, the Boy Wonderful" and the effect his secret identity was having on his love life. Sparrow's revelation at the end of the MAD piece, if applied to Burt Ward's Robin, might actually have had the effect of prolonging the life of the real *Batman* series. Sex sells, even in Gotham City!

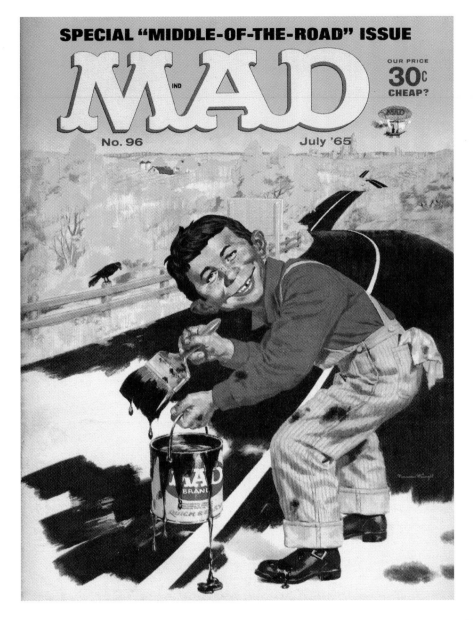

MAD

No. 96   July '65

OUR PRICE
30¢
CHEAP?

SPECIAL ALFRED OF ARABIA ISSUE

MAD

No. 96
April
'64

OUR PRICE
25¢
CHEAP

MAD

NO. 90   Oct. '64

OUR PRICE
25¢
CHEAP

FINK'S
DONUTS

MAD

No. 89 Sept. '64

OUR PRICE
25¢
CHEAP

MAD
MONSTER

MAD

No. 83   March '65

OUR PRICE
25¢
CHEAP

INTRODUCING
"THE MAD POLUYT"

SELF-PORTRAIT

WRITER & ARTIST: AL JAFFEE

"That's right, Operator! Long Distance– Person-to-Person to Arnold Finster–"

There goes crafty old
Arnold Finster—bilking
the Telephone Company
again by placing a
Long Distance
Person-to-Person
call to himself—
a free way to let
his family know
he arrived safely!

Maybe if we stopped spending millions of dollars for fancy ads like these to
get folks to phone Long Distance...and lowered our rates instead, guys like
Arnold Finster could afford to make legitimate Long Distance telephone calls!

BILKED TELEPHONE SYSTEM

*Calling yourself Person-to-Person is the
next best thing to calling Long Distance*

Make Beautiful Hair

B L E C C H

THERE ARE THREE BLECCH SHAMPOOS FOR THREE DIFFERENT HAIR CONDITIONS

Are you a teenage boy with Beautiful Hair? Well no wonder the girls hardly notice you. Today, you've got to be a teenage boy with Blecch hair. Then the girls will scream with delight, roll on the floor and kick their feet when they see you. So why waste another minute? Shampoo your hair with Blecch tonight. Blecch comes in three special formulas:

● For dry hair—a special formula that takes neat crew-cut type hair and lays it down over your ears. For oily hair —loosens up that slick-combing stuff so it spills down over your eyes. ● For normal hair—gives it proper body so it mushrooms all over your head. Get the shampoo that's right for you, and make your hair "Blecch"! Yeah! Yeah! Yeah!

I JUST PUT A GAS STATION ATTENDANT IN MY TANK!

"URP!"

'Clarke

MAINLY BECAUSE I GOT SICK AND TIRED OF BEING EXPLOITED!

1 First there was that idiotic Tiger on all them boxes of Sugar Frosted Flakes—used by

2 Then came them ads for those Tiger paw tires on Pontiac's GTO Tiger to sell you

3 Then there's that ridiculous broad lying all over the Tiger skin on TV for

4 And finally there's this stupid idea of putting a Tiger in your car's tank by using

WELL, THAT'S THE LAST STRAW! HONESTLY, I'M JUST FED UP WITH MADISON AVENUE'S PREOCCUPATION WITH TIGERS! NOW, MAYBE THEY'LL THINK TWICE BEFORE THEY COME OUT WITH ANOTHER ADVERTISING CAMPAIGN FEATURING ME!

THE REPLACEMENT

ARTIST: BOB CLARKE   WRITER: DON EDWING

Early One Morning In The Jungle

ARTIST: FRANK FRAZETTA   WRITER: DON EDWING

I'm the guy who puts eight great tomatoes in that little bitty can!!

All day long – squashing, squooshing, slamming, splattering . . . Yeccch, what a mess! Thank goodness it's my last week at this gooky job! Next week my company starts using a new-type can, and I'll be able to stuff those eight great tomatoes in that little bitty can without ending up looking like I've been attacked with a meat cleaver. Mainly because our new "little bitty can" expands into a "biggy wiggy can" like an accordion.

Concertina

EXPANDING CAN

Likely Strife separates the men from the boys...

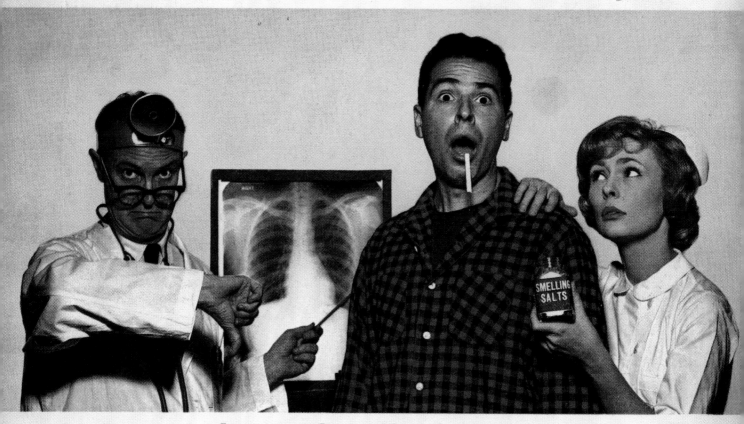

but not from the doctors.

Smoking is a habit we'd like to get all you kids hooked on.
Hey, kids! Wanna feel grown up? Wanna feel like a man?
Wanna be separated from the boys—but not from the girls?
Smoke Likely Strife—and you'll discover one other thing:
You'll also be separated from your health!

What have we got against colds?

Absolutely nothing! We love 'em!

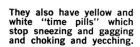

We manufacture capsules that have these tiny red "time pills" which stop sniffles and runny nose.

They also have yellow and white "time pills" which stop sneezing and gagging and choking and yecching.

These "time pills" don't actually cure the cold — they just suppress the symptoms so you feel good.

That's how we move plenty of these capsules. You go around spreading cold germs instead of staying in bed.

CONTACT ✗ *ALL DAY / ALL NIGHT GERM SPREADING*

SNIFF

We call this a "Time Capsule" because it gives you time to spread the cold.

1 CAPSULE EVERY 12 HOURS

will do nothing for you, but plenty for us. Because the more colds, the more capsules we'll move. Personal contact is needed to spread colds, but who's gonna be stupid enough to go near someone slobbering with a juicy cold? Nobody! That's why we created this tricky capsule. It makes colds **seem** to disappear—so

COLDS SPREAD ON
CONTACT
10 CONTINUOUSLY CONTAGIOUS CAPSULES—STOP SYMPTOMS, NOT GERMS

Today's largest selling substitute for legitimate prescription cold remedies.

MAD's Great Moments In Advertising

THE DAY THEY FORGOT TO PUT THE TOP DOWN FOR THE HERTZ COMMERCIAL

MAD's
Great Moments In Advertising

THE DAY THE WRONG GIANT CAME OUT OF THE WASHER— *HO-HO-HO!*

THE LITTLE WOODEN PUPPET
A Scene We'd Like to See

ARTIST: BOB CLARKE

Here is MAD's version of the Academy Award-winning movie that opens with a wild motorcycle ride taken by one of the most mysterious and confusing personalities in world history . . .

This motorcycle rider had once been a rough-and-tumble soldier, despite the fact that he was well-educated, well-mannered, dressed immaculately, and spoke with perfect diction . . .

Ooops!—Wrong motorcycle rider! Hey, you guys up in the projection booth! That's Marlon Brando in the opening scene from "The Wild One!" That was a character we **understood**! Not like

FLAWRENCE OF ARABIA

ARTIST: MORT DRUCKER   WRITER: LARRY SIEGEL

Have you heard? Flawrence of Arabia is dead! Tell me . . . what was he **really** like?

He was one of the greatest men in history!

He was a cad—a bounder—a fink!

He was a military genius!

He was a nut!

He was beautiful, sweetie!

He was sick!

He led a charmed life! He was indestructible!

So how come he got killed in a motorcycle crash?

All right, already! So let's make with the **flashbacks!** Like to British H.Q.—Cairo, Egypt—1917!

AND WHAT IS YOUR LAST NAME, MY DEAR? CHRISTINE---

MAD is often asked why it doesn't have expensive full-color three-page fold-outs the way other high-class magazines like "Life" and "Play-boy" have. There are two reasons for this! One: MAD is against osten-tatious, snobbish, status-seeking gimmicks, and Two: MAD is cheap! So here instead is our economy-minded black-and-white one-page

MAD FOLD-IN

FOLD PAGE OVER LIKE THIS

FOLD THIS SECTION OVER TO LEFT   FOLD THIS SECTION BACK TO RIGHT

Jaffee

Elizabeth Taylor, looking radiantly beautiful at the premiere of her latest film, is positively enchanted by

escort Richard Burton, who glows in the knowledge that he is the only one in her heart, and that she is his.

Meanwhile, people push and shove for autographs while police try to keep them in check! Hey! Take a look at

the handsome young stranger in the crowd moving in for his chance. Obviously, he's destined to be next in line.

Smoking has been linked with so many horrible sicknesses, you'd imagine that everybody would be giving it up. Not so! Most smokers simply cannot! And so—they are now doubly-plagued! Not only are they deteriorating physically from smoking, but mentally, too—from worrying about it. In order to help all these poor trapped souls, we now offer...

SOME MAD DEVICES FOR SAFER SMOKING

ARTIST & WRITER: AL JAFFEE

Cigarette smoking is largely a nervous habit in which the act of "lighting up" and "taking a deep drag" is more important than the actual smoke!—so say leading

DISPOSABLE LUNG-LINER TIPS

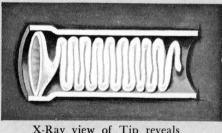

"Lung-Liner Tips" come in boxes of 20 to accommodate regular pack of cigarettes.

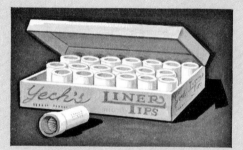

X-Ray view of Tip reveals folded plastic bag inside.

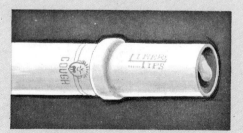

Liner Tip attaches to the cigarette, and looks just like a regular filter tip.

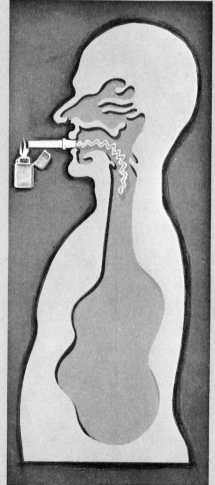

As smoker inhales, folded plastic liner is drawn down throat into lungs. Plastic is extremely thin, clings like Saran Wrap to insides.

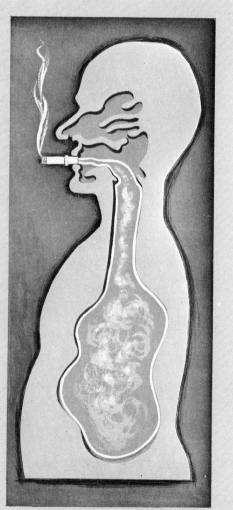

Thus, "Lung-Liner" transmits 90% of smoking's sensation with 100% safety. After use, liner is easily withdrawn for convenient disposal.

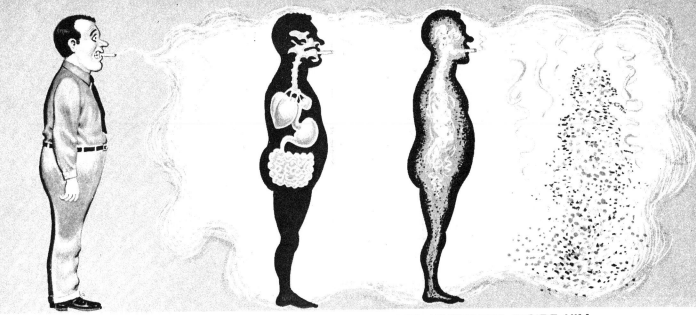

A SMOKER'S MENTAL PICTURE OF WHAT'S HAPPENING INSIDE HIM

psychologists. With this in mind, MAD has designed—and now offers—these devices which retain the main actions of smoking while eliminating the smoke itself...

PORTABLE FILTRATION UNITS

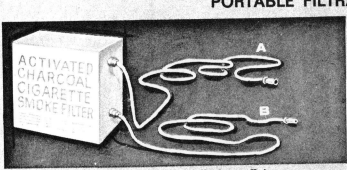

ACTIVATED CHARCOAL CIGARETTE SMOKE FILTER

"Filtration Unit" is small, but efficient version of a Military Gas Mask canister.

Close up of cross-section shows pinch-proof construction of tubes "A" and "B".

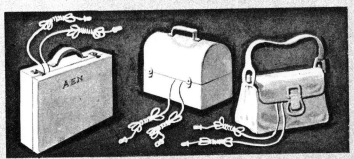

Filtration Units can be fitted into any number of portable containers, such as attache case, lunch box, handbag, etc.

In use, when smoker inhales, harmful smoke travels down from cigarette thru tube "A" to Filtration Unit, returns as pure fresh air thru tube "B" to healthy satisfied smoker.

SMOKE SIMULATORS

"Smoke Simulators" also come in boxes of 20 ... providing one for each cigarette.

Simulators are hollow Pyrex tubes filled with water "A" and corked at one end "B".

Inserted into cigarette, note how disc "C" blocks smoke, seals off end of cigarette.

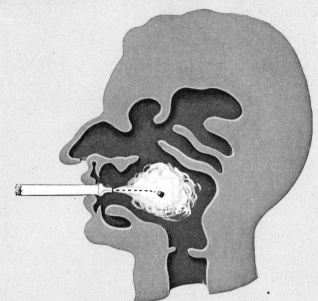

As smoker lights up, hot ash of cigarette boils water in Pyrex Simulator tube. Steam pops cork (which is made of edible material and can be swallowed safely). The steam feels just like smoke. Tests in dark rooms proved this: A smoker cannot distinguish between real smoke, hot air, or steam. Now, smoking with a cold (using Simulator) is not only enjoyable, but downright soothing and healing as well!

The following devices are for the confirmed smoker who must taste the real smoke if he is to be satisfied. For

NASAL EXHAUST FAN

Tiny "Nasal Exhaust Fan" (Note size of penny "A"!) has flesh-tone tubes and nose plugs "B".

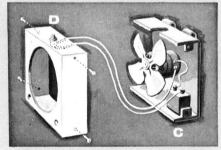

Tiny fan motor is powered by long-lasting battery "C" and is controlled by switch "D".

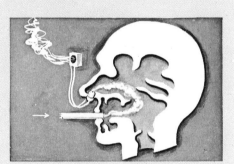

In operation, fan pulls smoke from cigarette up through nose, thus avoiding throat and lungs.

Attached to eyeglasses

Hidden in beard

Used like a hearing aid

There are many possible ways of wearing a "Nasal Exhaust Fan". A few are shown above. Main benefit of this device is: it keeps smoke from affecting hard-to-get-at throat and lungs. Nose cancer is much easier to reach and treat.

SMOKE-EJECTOR BULBS

"Smoke-Ejector Bulbs" are small balloon-like objects

They attach easily to the mouth end of any cigarette, filtered or unfiltered.

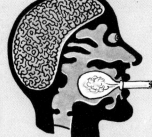

Smoker inserts cigarette— with "Smoke-Ejector Bulb" attached—into mouth, and lights cigarette normally.

As smoker begins to inhale, the Ejector Bulb begins to fill with smoke and expand.

Smoke-Ejector Bulb keeps on expanding as long as smoker is able to keep on inhaling.

If smoker releases tension, Bulb collapses and smoke is ejected without ever touching the inside of his mouth.

him, cutting down the amount and the intensity of smoke taken in may at least reduce the danger to some degree.

"HOT LIPS" DISCOURAGER

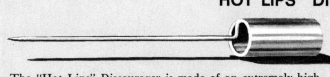

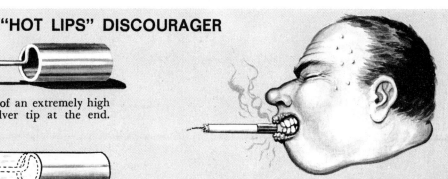

The "Hot Lips" Discourager is made of an extremely high heat-conducting silver rod with a silver tip at the end.

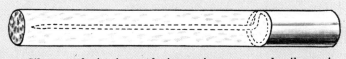

Silver rod is inserted into cigarette, and silver tip fits flush to cigarette-end like an expensive holder.

As smoker begins to puff, silver rod heats up fast and transmits heat to end which sears smoker's lips. Hardy smokers may stick till half the cigarette is gone, but average threshold of pain makes most quit ¼ way thru.

THE "PSYCHOLOGICAL WARFARE" INSERT

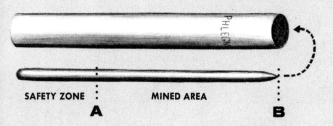

SAFETY ZONE   MINED AREA
A   B

This ingenious insert looks like a solid metal spike, but is actually hollow. Somewhere between **"A"** and **"B"** there is an explosive charge. When inserted into the center of the cigarette with the **"Safety Zone"** toward the end to be lit, it affords a short time to enjoy the smoke. However, any daring smoker who has the explosive charge blow up in his face usually never ventures past the **"Safety Zone"** again.

Smoker who almost waited too long before disposing of butt.

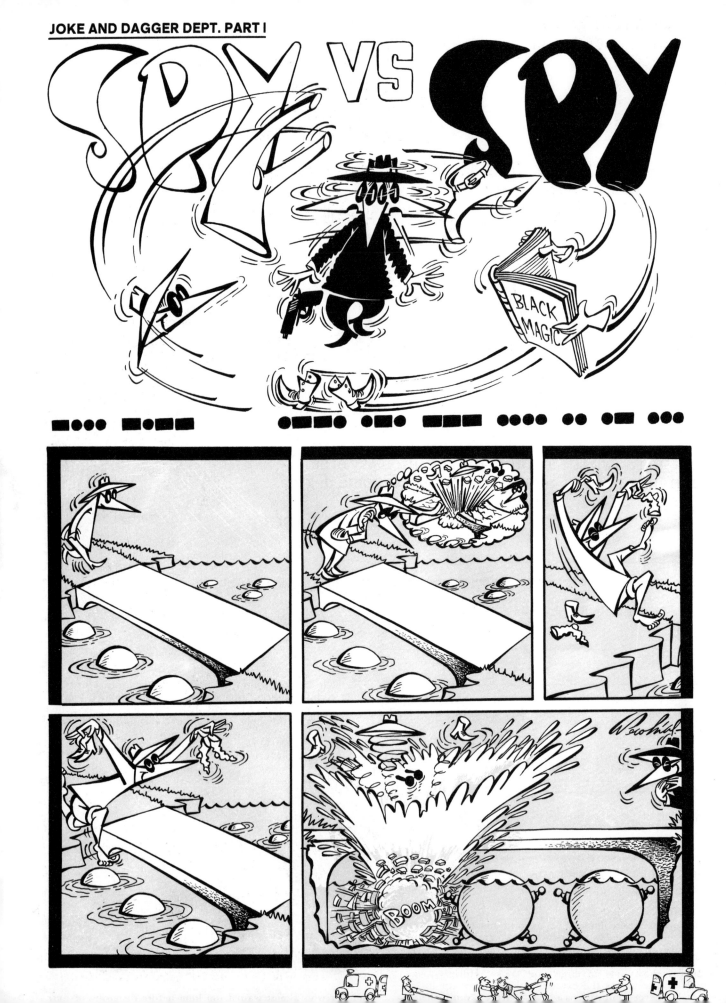

Continuing with its creative programming efforts, this past season ABC introduced a new addition to its "Doctor Show" and "Crime Show" TV trail-blazing . . . mainly a "Doctor-Crime Show" called:

THE PHEWGITIVE

ARTIST: MORT DRUCKER   WRITER: STAN HART

This is your stern-voiced narrator — Every week, we remind you of what the program is about, since you might not get the idea from the subtle title. We also kill 5 minutes of each show by using the same opening every week!

Dr. Richard Thimble is on his way to the Death House, convicted of murdering his wife. What thoughts are going through the head of the distinguished gray-haired physician at this moment?

As he stares into the night, contemplating the shafting he got from that Jury who wouldn't believe his story about the "one-armed man" — Fate steps into the life of Dr. Richard Thimble!

Instead of completing his journey, a curious event has made Dr. Richard Thimble a free man . . . free to run all over the country, searching for the "one-armed man", getting involved in people's lives, and narrowly escaping re-capture every week!

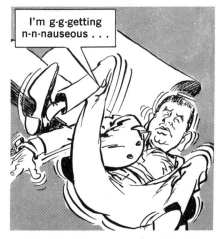

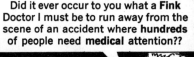

HERE WE GO AGAIN WITH OUR FICTIONALIZED VERSION OF THINGS WE'D PROBABLY FIND IF WE WERE TO EXAMINE THE CONTENTS OF

NAME: *Ringo Starr*

ADDRESS: *Liverpool, England*

OCCUPATION: *Ask any Teenage Girl!!*

IN CASE OF EMERGENCY, NOTIFY:

Parliament, the British Foreign Office, The Board of Inland Revenue & Ed Sullivan

THIS IS ME ~~WITH MY GIRL~~   THIS IS ME <u>WITH MY GIRL</u>

The Liverpool School Of Music

"The Sweetest Musicians This Side Of The Docks"

We regret to inform student ....RICHARD STARKEY....

that he has failed his course in ......D.R.U.M.S.......

for the school term beginning ...SEPT. '61... and ending ...FEB. '62...

Byron Harold Keats
Headmaster

(Sing) SHE LOVES YOU... YEAH, YEAH, YEAH!
 (*Hit my drums, shake my hair and wait for the screams*)
(Sing) SHE LOVES YOU... YEAH, YEAH, YEAH!
 (*Hit my drums, shake my hair and wait for more screams*)
(Sing) SHE LOVES YOU,.. YEAH, YEAH, YEAH-YEAH!
 (*Hit my drums, move my head from side to side and sneer*)
(Sing) WELL YOU THINK YOU'VE LOST YOUR LOVE
 (*Hit my drums, shake my hair, wait for screams and grin*)
(Sing) WELL I SAW HER YES-TER-DAY... YI, YAY!
 (*Hit my drums, shake my hair and say "Whooooo!"*)
(Sing) IT'S YOU SHE'S THINKING OF
 (*Look towards John for further instructions*)

From the desk of
MOE
"The Three Stooges"
205 Maurer Beach Drive
Hollywood, California

August 3rd, 1962

Dear Mr. Starr:

Thank you for your kind letter. You're the first one to compliment my hair comb in the last twenty years. Everyone else tells me how ridiculous I look. But what do I care? When they say it, I just kick 'em in the knee and bop 'em in the head.

As for your question about how I go about "doing my hair", it's very simple. I just comb it straight forward in bangs using water and a brush. Occasionally, if I want it to sparkle, I use seltzer.

Incidentally, why would you possibly want this information? Are you and your friends doing a scrapbook of me or something? Are you starting a fan club in England for me? If you want, I can send you photos of me smashing heads together. Or poking eyes out.

Let me know, kid.

Yours in subtle comedy,

Moe

MOE of "The Three Stooges"

Timmons & Hedgepot, Jewelers
"We Specialize In Rings Of All Kinds"
144 CHAUNCEY COURT, LIVERPOOL, LANCS. ENGLAND

INVOICE OF TRANSACTIONS TO DATE WITH: Mr. Ringo Starr			ACCT. NO. 78-5640
DATE	DESCRIPTION	COMMENT	PRICE
7/2/62	1 Captain Midnight Decoder Ring	For left pinky..	£2/-
11/12/62	1 Silver Ring (with squirter attachment)	For right forefinger	£2/8-
2/10/63	1 Gold Ring (imitation)	For left forefinger	£3/7-
6/23/63	1 Ruby Ring (synthetic)	For third finger of right hand..	£5/2-
11/9/63	1 Gold Ring (24 karats)	For third finger of left hand..	£8/-
9/5/63	1 Star Sapphire Ring	For left thumb..	£240/7-
1/14/64	1 Diamond Ring (5 karats)	For middle finger of right hand..	£18,000/-
7/8/64	1 Pearl Solitaire Ring (27 karats)	For big toe of left foot....	£67,000/3/
9/18/64	The Hope Diamond	To hang from right ear.....	£289,000/9/

A CELEBRITY'S WALLET

ARTIST: BOB CLARKE
WRITER: ARNIE KOGEN

The National Theatre Company

Formerly The Old Vic Company

Waterloo Road, London S.E. 1, England

Dear Ringo:--

We are in receipt of your letter expressing a desire to act in one of our Shakespeare productions.

Frankly, although we have never heard of you, we have studied the photograph of yourself that you sent us, and we think we may have a spot for you--as Ophelia in "Hamlet".

Thank you for thinking of us, Miss Starr, and please call so that we may arrange for an audition.

Sincerely,

Laurence O'Halivah

Laurence O'Halivah
Production Manager,
The National Theatre Company
(Formerly The Old Vic Company)

From The Desk Of
Brian Epstein

MANAGER TO "THE BEATLES"

Dear Ringo

I have given your request careful consideration and I have come to the conclusion that it would not be fair if you received more money than John or Paul or George.

Yes, I realize that as the drummer for the group, you play an important part that even the public is not aware of—but I do not feel that just because you carry the _melody_, you are entitled to more.

Regards—
Brian

Dear Ringo,

It was sweet of you to send me that "I Like Ringo Best" button and the Ringo Bubble Gum Cards. I know that you'd like to see more people wearing _your_ button, and I'd love to help you out, but as you must realize, it would be rather awkward for me to do so.

Best of luck anyway

Mrs John Lennon

HORNBLOWER, AINSWORTHY & GOODFINK
Solicitors

Picadilly, London W. I.

October 20, 1964

Mr. Ringo Starr
Liverpool, Lancs.

England

Dear Mr. Starr:--

We are herewith returning the tearsheet of the satirical ad from the back cover of MAD Magazine that you sent us.

As your Solicitors, it is our opinion that there is absolutely no cause for libel or for slander in this item. As a matter of fact, the portrait is quite flattering. You do look like that, you know!

Frankly, if we were you, we would consider ourselves lucky.

It could easily have been a "Does she...or doesn't she?" ad.

Sincerely yours,

Melvin Goodfink

Melvin Goodfink
for
Hornblower, Ainsworthy
Goodfink

MG/rr
1 encl.

Here we go with the 2nd of a three-part series on "Parties." Last issue we looked at "Adult Parties." Next issue we will cover "Kids' Parties." But this time, it's—

THE LIGHTER SIDE OF TEEN

Oh, Daddy! Can I throw a party for the gang?

How do you like that?! My daughter is growing up! She's thirteen, and wants to throw her own shindig! It reminds me of when **I** was thirteen . . .

. . . and I went to Adrian Burner's party! Boy, that was fun! She and I ended up in the backyard . . . **HEY, WAIT A MINUTE!!**

CERTAINLY NOT!!

Are you **working?** How much do you **make** a week?

What does your **father** do?

I—er—

What do you plan on **becoming**—a doctor, a lawyer, an engineer, **what?**

Well—I—er—

Does your family intend setting you up in **business?**

Can you **support** a family?

Has there ever been any **insanity** in your family?

Gee—I—uh—

Honest, folks, I just happened to be the **first guest** to show up at your daughter's **party!** I really hadn't **planned** on getting **married** tonight!

Hey, **quiet** everybody! Quick! Turn out the **lights!** Here come those **Mepham High Boys**, looking to crash this party!

Oh-oh! They're stopping!

I can't understand how they **always know** exactly where there's a **party** to crash!

MEPHAM HIGH CRASHERS
THIS IS THE PLACE

PARTY!

20 DOLL GIRLS COUNT 'EM 20

ASK FOR MARTHA SUE BOBBI GAY LAURIE PAM RUTH

30 CLOD BOYS FORGET 'EM! 30

GET RID OF FRANK, ANDY, STEVE, NORMAN

FUN! FUN!

AGE PARTIES

ARTIST & WRITER: DAVE BERG

IN THE DELICATESSEN

Since MAD's Official Article-Introduction Writer is ill this month, we've assigned Sidney Gwirtzman, MAD's Accountant, to serve as Guest Introduction Writer for the following article. Here is Mr. Gwirtzman's Introduction: *"The law provides a credit against tax dividends received from qualifying domestic corporations. This credit is equal to 4 percent of these dividends in excess of those which you may exclude from your income. The credit may not exceed: (a) the total income tax reduced by foreign tax credit; or (b) 4 percent of the . . ."* But enough of this hilarity. Let's save the jokes for the story as

MAD LOOKS AT A TYPICAL
KIDDIE TV SHOW

ARTIST: MORT DRUCKER   WRITER: LARRY SIEGEL

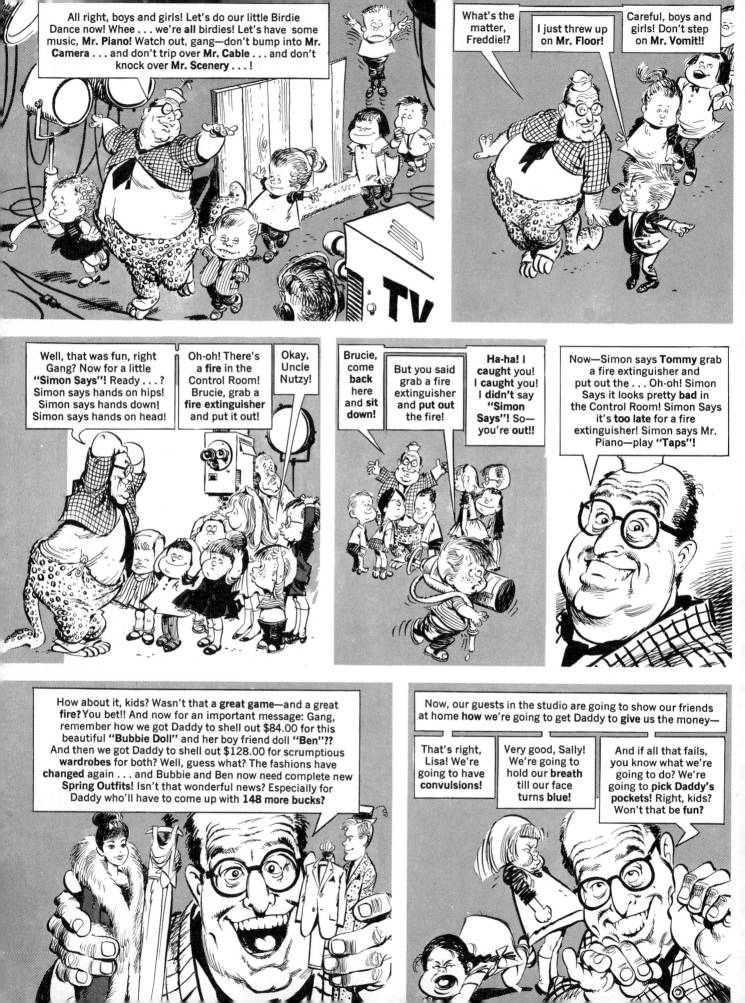

For years, the nation's educators have been howling about the evils inherent in such big time college sports as football and basketball. They contend that there's too much professionalism, that not enough boys have a chance to participate, etc. But no one really lifted a finger to correct the situation until MAD's Athletic Council went to work—and he's come up with a brand new sport that promises to provide good, clean amateur fun for all. Here, then, are the rules for this great new national pastime of the future. Digest them carefully and be the last person in your neighborhood to play ... as ...

MAD MAGAZINE
introduces
43-MAN SQUAMISH

ARTIST: GEORGE WOODBRIDGE   WRITER: TOM KOCH

A Squamish team consists of 43 players: the left & right Inside Grouches, the left & right Outside Grouches, four Deep Brooders, four Shallow Brooders, five Wicket Men, three Offensive Niblings, four Quarter-Frummerts, two Half-Frummerts, one Full-Frummert, two Overblats, two Underblats, nine Back-Up Finks, two Leapers and a Dummy.

Each player is equipped with a long hooked stick known as a Frullip. The Frullip is used to halt opposing players attempting to cross your goal line with the Pritz (ball). The Official Pritz is 3¾ inches in diameter and is made of untreated Ibex hide stuffed with Blue Jay feathers.

Play begins with the Probate Judge flipping a new Spanish peseta. If the Visiting Captain calls the toss correctly, the game is immediately cancelled. If he fails to call it correctly, then the Home Team Captain is given his choice of either carrying the Pritz ... or defending against it.

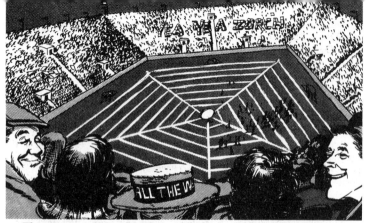

The game of Squamish is played on a 5-sided field known as a Flutney. The two teams line up at opposite sides of the Flutney and play seven Ogres of fifteen minutes each — unless it rains, in which case they play eight Ogres.

The defending right Outside Grouch signifies that he is ready to hurl the Pritz by shouting, "Mi Tio es infermo, pero la carretera es verde!"—a wise old Chilean proverb that means, "My Uncle is sick, but the highway is green!"

The offensive team, upon receiving the Pritz, has five Snivels in which to advance to the enemy goal. If they do it on the ground, it's a Woomik and counts 17 points. If they hit it across with their Frullips, it's a Durmish which only counts 11 points. Only the offensive Niblings and Overblats are allowed to score in the first 6 Ogres.

Special rules, applicable only during the seventh Ogre, turn the game into something very akin to Buck Euchre. During this final Ogre (and the eighth, if it rains), the four Quarter-Frummerts are permitted to either kick or throw the Pritz, and the nine Finks are allowed to heckle the opposition by doing imitations of Barry Goldwater.

A typical seventh Ogre play is shown below. Team "A"— trailing 516—209, is in possession of the Pritz with fourth Snivel and half the Flutney to go. Suddenly, the left Underblat, going for the big one, sends two Shallow Brooders and the Full-Frummert downfield. Obviously, he is going to try for a Woomik when the opposition expects a Durmish. A daring play of this type invariably brings the crowd rising to its feet and heading for the exits.

A variety of penalties keep play from getting out of hand. Walling the Pritz, Frullip-gouging, icing on fifth Snivel, running with the mob and raunching are all minor infractions subject to a ten-yard penalty. Major infractions (sending the Dummy home early, interfering with Wicket Men, rushing the season, bowing to the inevitable and inability to face facts) are punishable by loss of half the Flutney, except when the Yellow Caution Flag is out.

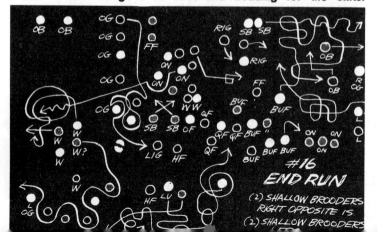

Squamish rules provide for 4 officials: a Probate Judge, a Field Representative, a Head Cockswain and a Baggage Smasher. None has any authority after play has begun. In the event of a disagreement between the officials, a final decision is left up to the spectator who left his car in the parking lot with the lights on and the motor running.

In the event of a tie score, the teams play a sudden-death overtime. The exception to this rule occurs when opposing Left Overblats are both out of the game on personal fouls. When such is the case, the two teams line up on opposite sides of the Flutney and settle the tie by shouting dirty limericks at each other until one team breaks up laughing.

Amateur Squamish players are strictly forbidden to accept subsidies, endorse products, make collect phone calls or eat garlic. Otherwise, they lose their amateur standing. A player may turn Pro, however, merely by throwing a game.

Schools with small enrollments which preclude participation in 43-Man Squamish may play a simplified version of the game: 2-Man Squamish. The rules are identical, except that in 2-Man Squamish, the object of the game is to lose.

The original charter calls for an annual meeting of the National Squamish Rules Committee. At its inaugural meeting, the committee approved a re-wording of Article XVI, Paragraph 77, Section J of the rules. This section, which formerly read: "The offensive left Underblat, in all even-numbered Ogres, must touch down his Frullip at the edge of the Flutney and signal to the Head Cockswain that he is ready for play to continue," has now been simplified

to read: "The offensive left Underblat, in all even-numbered ogres, must touch down his Frullip at the edge of the Flutney and signal to either the Head Cockswain, or to any other official to whom the Head Cockswain may have delegated this authority in writing and in the presence of two witnesses, both of whom shall have been approved and found to be of high moral character by the Office of the Commissioner, that he is ready for play to continue."

Are you plagued by clods who ask stupid questions? We mean the kind of questions to which the answers are painfully obvious. Doesn't it drive you nuts to have to give such answers? Don't you wish you could come up with snappy answers that would put these dolts down, like the comics on TV always do? Well, you can! All you need is a sense of humor, a little practice, and a mean, rotten disposition. You also need to convince yourself that there is

MAD'S SNAPPY ANSWERS

No, thanks! I already **have** one!

No, I'm a **modern sculptor!**

No, I'm starting a **junk yard!**

No, I'm doing **The Frug!**

No, I'm studying to be a **kangaroo!**

No, I'm hitchhiking to the **bathroom!**

No, it's the **beginning!** We're all **facing backwards!**

No, it's the end of a **freight train,** and I'm the **caboose!**

No, it's a group of **casual strollers,** who, by some **fantastic coincidence,** have come to stand one behind the other at this **one spot!**

----

nothing worse than stupid clods who ask pointless unnecessary questions. Is that clear? Do you understand what we mean? Are we getting the point of this article across to you? Isn't this the perfect time to come up with one of them snappy answers? Okay! Study the typical situations on these pages and practice giving the snappy answers we've printed. Then start making up your own. Before long you'll see how gratifying it is to humiliate people with ....

TO STUPID QUESTIONS

ARTIST & WRITER: AL JAFFEE

We've had preposterous "Private Eye" characters in literature (Mickey Spillane's "Mike Hammer")! And we've had preposterous "Secret Agent" characters in movies (Ian Fleming's "James Bond")! But now we've got the most preposterous "Private Eye-Secret Agent" character of them all—on the most preposterous medium of them all—television! We're talking about the guy on the weekly NBC-TV show called

THE MAN FROM A.U.N.T.I.E.

On a street in the East 50's in New York City, there is an ordinary Tailor Shop! We entered through the Agent's Entrance . . .

Isn't this a **clever concept**— having an ordinary Tailor Shop as the **secret entrance** to our **secret Headquarters Building?**

So . . . if it's **so clever,** why is our "Nielsen Rating" only 16.8??

We passed the ordinary-looking tailor pressing ordinary-looking dresses—crossed to the back room—and pulled open the drapes!

ARTIST: MORT DRUCKER   WRITER: ARNIE KOGEN

EEEEEK!

What's the idea of undressing in the back room of this ordinary Tailor Shop in the East 50's— which is actually the secret entrance to the secret Headquarters Building of A.U.N.T.I.E.!

Idiots! Clods! Dolts! The ordinary Tailor Shop you A.U.N.T.I.E. guys want is in the **EAST 40's**—not the East 50's! Everybody in New York knows that! You've got the **WRONG SHOP!**

HORROR Movie Scenes We'd Like To See

ARTIST: JACK DAVIS   WRITER: DON EDWING

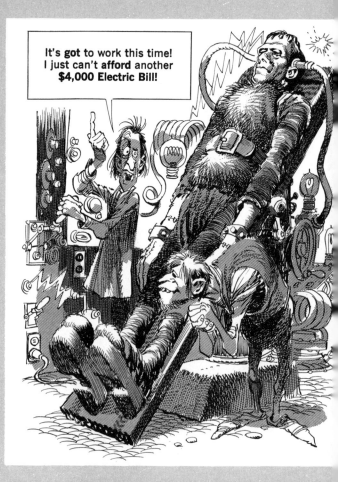

A BOY and his CHEMISTRY SET

Junior!? What are you **doing??**

Gad! It's my **Mother!**

Nothing, Mom... just playing with my chemistry set!

Everybody's going wild over that new TV show featuring "The Caped Crusader" and his teenage side-kick. But has anyone ever wondered what it would really be like as the side-kick of a "Caped Crusader"? Would a typical red-blooded teenage boy really be happy dressing in some far-out costume and spending all of his free time chasing crooks? Or would he much prefer dressing in chinos and go-go boots and spending all of his free time chasing chicks? We at MAD think the latter! In fact, we're ready to prove it! Let's take a MAD look at "Boy Wonderful" as he is slowly being driven

BATS-MAN

ARTIST: MORT DRUCKER   WRITER: LOU SILVERSTONE

Finster Cleaners? This is **Bats-Man!** You sent me the **wrong** costume! What do you mean "You sent it to the **ballet school** by mistake"? Get it back and send it over to me **quick!**

You'd sure look **ridiculous** fighting crime in **this** outfit, Mr. Swain!

Meanwhile, at Franklin D. Wilson High School...

Hi, Zelda. Would you like to go to the dance with me Saturday night?

I already have a date with the captain of the ping-pong team! You can't expect a girl to be seen with a **non-athletic** type like **you**, Gray Dickson!

Hi, Candy. How about going to the dance with me?

You've got a lot of **nerve** asking me for a date after what happened the **last** time I went out with you, Gray Dickson! Ditching me for a **middle-aged lady!** I saw you **sneaking off** down the back staircase with her!

Holy Tony Curtis! That was no **lady**—that was **Bats-Man!** He came to get me when "The Kibitzer" escaped from jail! This "Boy Wonderful" bit is really lousing up my **love life!** I'm going to have to straighten a few things out!

Summer 1967: The Summer of Love is upon us. Psychedelia is in. The record spinning on seemingly everyone's turntable is *Sgt. Pepper's Lonely Hearts Club Band* by the Beatles. President Lyndon Johnson has just announced plans to send 45,000 more troops into Vietnam. Use of mind-expanding drugs is at an all-time high (pun intended); by the summer of 1969 man will be literally on the moon.

The "take a trip/banana peel" cover of issue #116 (January 1968) is in reference to a widely repeated but false rumor in circulation at the time that the scrapings from the inside of banana peels, properly cured and then smoked, would produce a "mellow yellow" high. The Don Martin piece that appears later in this section ("A San Francisco Trip") is a variation on this theme.

Another drug-culture-related cover appears on issue #118 (April 1968), lampooning Timothy Leary's "Turn On, Tune In, Drop Out" slogan. Leary is the ex–Harvard professor who became the undisputed guru and champion of the hallucinogen LSD. Leary gets the MAD treatment again in the "Celebrity's Wallet" piece that appears later in this section, from issue #116 (January 1968), written by Arnie Kogen.

Yet another guru also became cover material: the Maharishi Mahesh Yogi. Hailing from India, the Maharishi (an adopted name meaning "great soul") espoused Transcendental Meditation as the true path to inner peace and developed a huge following in the late sixties. In 1968, the Beatles, Mia Farrow, and Mike Love of the Beach Boys all sequestered themselves at the Maharishi's retreat in Rishakesh, India, to study T.M. John Lennon and Mike Love in particular responded favorably to the discipline. Lennon stayed almost three months in the ashram, until it was alleged that the Maharishi had made improper sexual advances toward one of the female meditators. All things considered, MAD evidently thought Alfred would make just as good a guru and presented this notion on the cover of issue #121 (September 1968). Lennon came to a similar conclusion and wrote the vitriolic "Sexy Sadie" (original title: "Maharishi") on the Beatles' "White Album" to commemorate the folly.

The cover of issue #122 (October 1968, but on newsstands in August), with Alfred holding balloons with the faces of political figures, had to be changed at press time. The cover originally had Robert Kennedy in the balloon at top right. Alfred's face was substituted at the last minute after Robert Kennedy was shot and killed on June 6, 1968, following a speech at the Ambassador Hotel in Los Angeles.

Incredibly, the "back to colege issue" cover of issue #131 (December 1969) brought scores of letters from readers pointing out that the word "isue" was spelled wrong, completely ignoring the spelling on "colege."

The "Great Moments in Politics" page was inspired by the gall bladder operation Lyndon Johnson had in 1967. Johnson, who by all accounts was a crass individual, was photographed showing his scar to newsmen. Writer Max Brandel saw the picture and had the inspired idea of superimposing a map of Vietnam onto Johnson's stomach.

In one of the few instances of an advertising-related parody appearing on a MAD front cover, the "We Don't Try Very Hard" button on the cover of issue #115 (December 1967) is a play on the long-running Avis Rent-A-Car "We Try Harder" ad campaign.

The "Ronreagan" ad spoofs both "Ronrico" rum and Ronald Reagan's failed bid for the 1968 Republican presidential nomination. Beaten but not defeated, Reagan turned it around and was elected President in 1980 in a landslide victory over President Jimmy Carter.

Dr. Seuss (Theodor Seuss Geisel) released the first *Cat in the Hat* book in 1957. By the mid-sixties he was probably the best-known and most successful author of children's books. Larry Siegel's brilliantly adult spin on Dr. Seuss ("The Cats Are All Bats") is accompanied by Bob Clarke's expert mimicry of Geisel's whimsical drawing style.

"Hokum's Heroes," by Siegel and Davis, is a disturbingly effective piece that shines a harsh light on this sitcom's conceit: that life for Nazi prison camp POW's could be some kind of zany, wacky adventure, and that the Germans were nothing more than bumbling, endearing idiots. Truth be told, when selecting the material for this book there was concern from the publisher that the piece might too harsh and too easily misinterpreted to include. Ultimately it was concluded that the really disturbing fact was not MAD's parody of the show, but rather that such a premise could get made even as a pilot for a series, let alone be put on the the air as comedy entertainment that actually pulled good ratings.

"Comic Strip Heroes Taken from Real Life," by Jacobs and Clarke, pokes fun at Johnson, Taylor and Burton, Hefner, Charles de Gaulle, Bob Dylan, Liberace, Barbra Streisand, and the boxer Cassius Clay. The strip on Clay refers to his draft resistance as a conscientious objector. Clay would later convert to the Muslim religion and change his name to one more familiar today: Muhammed Ali.

"Star Blecch" satirizes the quintessential science fiction TV show of the sixties, *Star Trek*. The show ran only three seasons (1966–1968) but has in the years since become a worldwide phenomenon, spawning many theatrical motion pictures and a host of spinoffs. The "transporter" sequence at the bottom of the second page is classic and prime MADness.

Arnie Kogen's "Hippie—the Magazine That Turns You On" (illustrated by George Woodbridge) contains several kilos' worth of high-grade satire and bears careful scrutiny, perhaps with kaleidoscopic glasses. Favorite blurb on the cover: "Is Free Love Worth It?" Kogen, incidentally, has continued down the sixties path of self-enlightenment. To that end, he now has a standing once-yearly appointment with his analyst. Once a year? "I get the full hour," Kogen explains.

"You Know You're Really a Parent When . . ." reminds us that while the country was seemingly being torn asunder by insane cultural and political changes, people were still going about the business of living their lives and raising their families. The piece was illustrated by Paul Coker, Jr., a longtime MAD contributor whose work will also be familiar to regular browsers of greeting card racks.

There is perhaps no other time in history when hair was as important as it was in the sixties. Hair that was too short instantly identified one as a "straight," and hair too long could get you kicked out of school or kept out of Disneyland. Dave Berg's "Lighter Side of Hair" examines hair from all angles, including the lack thereof.

"A Psychedelic Diary" was written by Dick DeBartolo, who does not smoke, drink, or take drugs. He does admit to being a notorious junk food junkie and reports that this piece was written on a sugar high induced by "two Pepperidge Farm mocha cakes and a package of Oreos." Incidentally, while MAD maintained an anti–substance abuse stance, it could hardly get too "preachy": John Putnam's first "Arthur" plant was not grown from an avocado seed but rather the seeds of something a little more smokable, and a lot more illegal.

2001: A Space Odyssey is Stanley Kubrick's groundbreaking and epic 1968 film about . . . well, a lot of people still aren't quite sure what it's about. Some mainstream critics panned the film, but it found its audience among the youth. Especially revered was the ending sequence, which was said to be even "trippier" if viewed when under the influence of a "mind-expanding" substance. Many moviegoers, however, found the film slow-moving and incomprehensible, which is where DeBartolo's MAD parody, "201 Min. of a Space Idiocy," comes in.

The *Mod Squad*, which ran from 1968 to 1973, was one of television's first attempts at "relevance." The series premise, about rebellious, young, and "hip" undercover cops, was suitably skewered by MAD as the "Odd Squad." *Mod Squad* was among the first TV shows produced by Aaron Spelling, who would later make a bazillion dollars producing such shows as *Charlie's Angels, Beverly Hills 90210,* and *Melrose Place.*

One of the most popular TV shows among the youthful in the late sixties was *The Smothers Brothers Comedy Hour.* Starring the harmless-enough-looking Tommy and Dick Smothers, the show ran from 1967 to 1969, when it was abruptly canceled by the network. After numerous ongoing and bitter battles between the Smothers and the CBS censors over the show's antiwar and antiestablishment slant, the network had had enough and pulled the plug. The "Smothered Brothers" piece predates this cancellation by almost a year and proved to be an ominous warning of things to come.

We conclude our time-capsule journey with Jacobs's and Aragonés's tribute to "Woodstock," the last great touchstone of the Age of Aquarius. You are now entering the seventies: smiley faces, the energy crisis, disco music, Watergate, *Star Wars,* and double-digit inflation.

But that's another book. Have a nice day!

—Grant Geissman

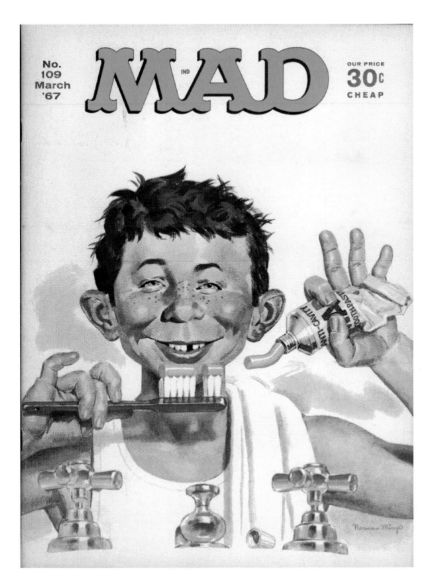

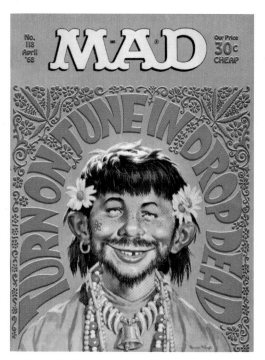

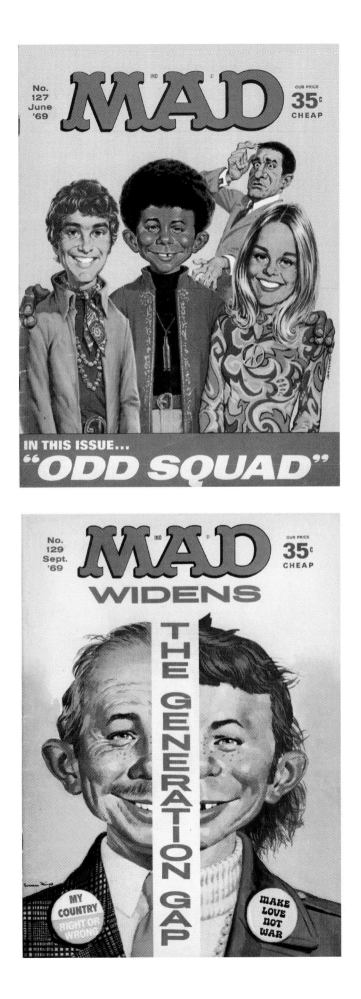

MAD

SPECIAL RACIAL ISSUE

No.
111
June
'67

OUR PRICE
30¢
CHEAP

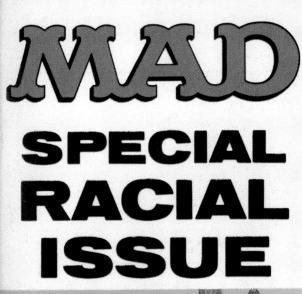

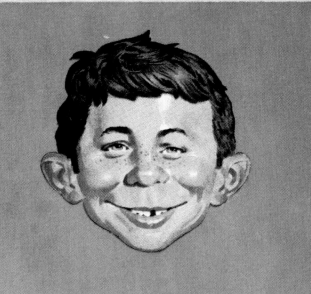

Norman Mingo

MAD's Great Moments In Politics

The further she is ... the closer you should look!*

Photography by Irving Schild

Scenes We'd Like To See

ARTIST: JACK RICKARD   WRITER: DON EDWING

Pinocchio

The Wizard of Oz

Peter Pan

THE BEAT GENERATION

ARTIST & WRITER: SERGIO ARAGONES

The 60-second disappointment

It happens too often with a Parloraid Color Pack Camera! That's why we can't take a chance. We photograph these <u>ads</u> with a Nikon loaded with Ektachrome!

Photography by Irving Schil

WHICH MODERN ARTIST IS MOST SUCCESSFULLY COMMUNICATING WITH HIS AUDIENCE?

HERE WE GO WITH ANOTHER RIDICULOUS
MAD FOLD-IN

"Modern Art" has taken some pretty wild turns in recent years. But no matter which direction it takes, it seems to be headed more and more toward total incomprehensibility. Reactions like "What is it?" and "What does it mean?" are almost guaranteed. But there is one modern artist whose work is understood by everyone! To find out who this phenomenal genius is, fold page in as shown.

FOLD PAGE OVER LIKE THIS!

A▶ FOLD THIS SECTION OVER LEFT **◀B** FOLD BACK SO "A" MEETS "B"

MANY MODERN ARTISTS HAVE LONG FELT THAT GREAT ART NEED NOT NECESSARILY BE UNDERSTOOD BY THE GENERAL PUBLIC, AND SOME HIDEOUS GROTESQUERIES HAVE BEEN CREATED IN THIS BELIEF!

ARTIST & WRITER: AL JAFFEE

A▶   **◀B**

Ron Reagan. Isn't he the ex-movie star who wanted to be President?

Yep! And it's something most folks would like to forget! That things like this are happening here in America! That old-time movie stars who weren't even that good in the first place have become Senators and Governors and yes— even made bids for Presidential nominations. It's enough to drive a thinking person to drink!

Ronreagan.   A rum to help forget.

RIGHT WING LABEL

RONREAGAN
PUERTO
REAGAN
RUM

In recent years, some of the most popular books for children have been among the series written and illustrated by Dr. Seuss. Now, as much as we admire Dr. Seuss and his strange looking creatures, his lilting rhymes and his inspired nonsense, we still can't seem to get very excited about "Zeds" and "Gacks" and "Seven-Hump Wumps." We figure it's about time for Dr. Seuss to face reality and turn his talents toward more meaningful stuff. In other words, we'd really like to see something like this . . .

ARTIST: BOB CLARKE   WRITER: LARRY SIEGEL

From there to here,
and here to there,
we all are sniffing
Poison Air.

We knew a man whose name was Cliff.
Of city air, he took a whiff.
He didn't have a handkerchief
to strain that air he chanced to sniff.
The sniff he took was quite terrif,
and now poor Cliff is cold and stiff.

Who are you
with that funny head?
What is your name?
Is it Fred or Red?
No, no, no!
My name's Con Ed.
I foul the air that made Cliff dead.

CONSOLIDATED EDISON

DIG WE MUST!

DIG?

But I'll be punished,
I can tell.
A hundred bucks
they'll fine me well.
A second's income
shot to hell!

Look at the hawk.
It's a hawk that can talk.
Would you like to be talked to
by a hawk?

Who is he?
He's General Cole.
He has a dream,
he has a goal,
to solve a problem
that tries Man's soul.

Here is the plan
of General Cole:
He wants to blow
a great big hole
into the Earth
from Pole to Pole.
It's the Army's answer
to Birth Control.

Up and down,
here and there,
Automation's
everywhere.

We met a man
whose name was Gene.
His Private Sec.
was a machine.
It typed for him
and answered phones,
and sat on his lap
and broke twelve bones.

"Let's wed," Gene said,
"You'll be my wife.
"You're not too soft,
but, well—that's life."

They wed and Gene
came home quite late
(his shirt all smudged)
to an angry mate,
who saw his collar
and began to boil,
and left him, saying
"That's not MY oil!"

Hark! Hark!
There is Clark
in the park.
Clark's in the park
after dark,
and he's being mugged.
What an easy mark!

As Clark yells out,
three cops take flight,
and six other people
run out of sight.

But along comes a man,
whose name is Dunn,
who isn't the kind
to turn and run.
He pitches right in,
kicks Clark in the crotch,
and helps himself
to Clark's Benrus watch.

Said Clark before
his scene dissolved,
"It wasn't much,
but he got involved!"

Say hello
to sweet Annette.
Annette has got
a lovely pet.
That's her pet—
its name's Yvette.

Who needs a Husband
to sit and fret,
to bet and sweat
and make you upset?
And who needs kids
to forget and wet?
Husbands and kids
can be a threat.
Which is why Annette
is in debt to her pet.
Yvette has never
talked back yet.

Each day Annette
will take Yvette
to a Dog Beauty Shop
for a Pet Hair Set
(With a set net, yet!)
And after Yvette
has had her set
Annette will take her
to the Vet.

Tell me, tell me—
How sick can you get?

His name is Bract
and he's got an Act
which is really great,
and that's a fact.

Now Bract can't decide
on a Ted Mack date,
or to run for President
in '68.

I LIKE ME

Bract stands on his head
with his feet in the air,
and clicks his heels
while he sings, "My Prayer".
Then he clacks three spoons
on the bones of his knee,
while his tongue on his teeth
clucks out "Marie".

We know a punk
whose name is Yunk.
They put him in jail
for killing a Monk.

He wasn't told
by Officer Wunk
to call his lawyer,
Bernie Schtunk.

His legal rights had
therefore shrunk,
so his confession
was deemed "bunk",
and in the street
he went, ker-plunk.

So if you're caught
while pushing "junk",
or stuffing someone
in a trunk,
and you are worried
that you're sunk,
remember the tale
of the punk
named Yunk.

In Winter, Summer,
Fall and Spring,
some funny things
are happening.

Loving, kissing,
billing, cooing.
Who knows what
they'll soon be doing?
Wife and Husband,
Father and Mother,
both are married—
but not to each other.

IRVING'S
Furs

There is this thing:
She's called a Wife.
She loves a Husband
all her life.
There is this Husband
loved by her,
who's bringing her
a fancy fur.

HEY, GANG . . . JOIN US NOW AS MAD PRESENTS ITS VERSION OF THE FUNNIEST SHOW ON TELEVISION SINCE THE "APPALACHIAN POVERTY SPECIAL." WE'RE TALKING ABOUT THE WEEKLY TV SITUATION COMEDY FEATURING THAT GAY, WILD, ZANY, IRREPRESSIBLE BUNCH OF WORLD WAR II PW'S . . . THOSE HAPPY INMATES OF "STALAG 14" KNOWN AS

HOKUM'S HEROES

MAD'S *Modern Believe It or Nuts!*

ARTIST: BOB CLARKE   WRITER: ARNIE KOGEN

Think Modern

LEGALIZE POT

Sandy Gloppslinger

...A BEARDED GREENWICH VILLAGE INTELLECTUAL WHO WEARS DIRTY WHITE SNEAKERS, HORN-RIMMED GLASSES AND BLUE JEANS... HAS PARTICIPATED IN EVERY PROTEST MARCH and RALLY HELD THERE... AND YET, HAS NEVER BURNED A DRAFT CARD!

...THAT'S BECAUSE SANDY GLOPPSLINGER IS A GIRL! She did, however, set fire to her beard once, in protest!

A FRATERNITY BACHELOR STAG PARTY WAS HELD FOR EUGENE FURD AT SYRACUSE UNIVERSITY... AND TO THE AMAZEMENT of the GUESTS PRESENT, A NAKED GIRL DID NOT JUMP OUT OF THE

CAKE!

EUGENE'S FRAT COULDN'T AFFORD A HUGE CAKE! THEY DID, HOWEVER, MANAGE TO GET A SMALL GIRL TO JUMP NAKED OUT OF A CHEESE DANISH!

CONTRARY TO POPULAR BELIEF... **ITALIAN MEN** DO NOT PINCH AMERICAN WOMEN *ONLY* ON THE VIA VENETO

...THEY PINCH THEM ALL OVER!

HIRAM ALBERT, 65 YEARS OF AGE, RETIRED TO FLORIDA ON $300 A MONTH... AND WAS ACTUALLY ABLE TO LIVE DECENTLY ON THAT AMOUNT!

ON JANUARY 12th, 1966, ON THE NBC TONIGHT SHOW, **JOHNNY CARSON** TOLD A JOKE... AND HIS SIDEKICK, **ED McMAHON** DID NOT GET HYSTERICAL!

ED WAS ON VACATION AT THE TIME...AND WAS BEING REPLACED BY JACK HASKELL...WHO DID NOT GET HYSTERICAL EITHER!

HIRAM ALBERT IS THE ALLIGATOR IN THE PICTURE ABOVE! HIS OWNER, SEEN WITH HIM, DIED OF STARVATION WITHIN A YEAR!

Eight years ago, MAD came up with a great idea—namely that Newspaper Syndicates might do well to create Comic Strips based on real people! Naturally, like most of the great ideas in MAD, it was completely ignored! Well, we still think it's a great idea — and even though we know we'll be ignored again, here's a brand new, up-to-date-selection of

Comic Strip Heroes

TAKEN FROM REAL LIFE

ARTIST: BOB CLARKE   WRITER: FRANK JACOBS

BIG LYNDON

THE BEAUTIFUL BURTONS

HEFNER AND HIS PALS

CHARLIE DE GAULLE IN PARIS

BOBBY DYLAN AND HIS GUITAR

LOVELY LIBERACE

BARBRA, THE BELTER

"I'd **love** teaming up with you, Ringo, but I have a feeling the Public might not be able to tell us **apart**!"

CASSIUS CLAY, HEAVYWEIGHT CHAMP

**The Beer Barrel Fox Trot

"THESE ARE THE VOYAGES OF THE STAR-SHIP 'BOOBY-PRIZE'! ITS MISSION, TO EXPLORE STRAN

HERE WE GO WITH ANOTHER "MAD" VERSION OF THE CONTENTS OF...
A CELEBRITY'S WALLET

WRITER:
ARNIE KOGEN

My darling Timmy,

What's happening to my son?

You used to be such a nice sensible boy--a college professor at Harvard--I was so proud of you. But now you've changed. I don't understand you any more. What's gotten into you?

I write you a civil letter asking how you are--and all I get back is a package of sugar cubes and a note filled with nonsense about "freak outs" and "vibrations" and "visions" and "voyages" and "expanding spiritual horizons". I'll expand your spiritual horizons for you-- right over your head! You keep this up and I'll come to Millbrook and give you such vibrations, you'll see visions for two weeks from my vibrations.

So you'd better shape up and be a good boy. And remember, no matter what kind of trouble you're in, I still love you. I know that basically you never meant any harm.

Mother

P.S. I just had my tea -- and I used your sugar cubes! Whooooopie!!

Copake Church Supply Co.
Peekskill, New York

Dr. Timothy Leary
Minister
League for Spiritual Discovery
Millbrook, N.Y.

Dear Dr. Leary:

Thank you for your recent order. We supply church equipment for all major religious denominations and, although we have not pre- viously heard of your "League for Spiritual Discovery", we will make every effort to meet your specifications. Shipment should be completed within 3-4 weeks.

However, there is one unusual item that disturbs us. Perhaps you will be good enough to satisfy our curiosity. We don't know what kind of services you conduct, but would you please explain why you ordered pews with <u>seat belts</u>?

Sincerely yours,

Millard Traymore

Millard Traymore
Sales Director

J. Walter Doyle & Dane Bernbach Thompson
ADVERTISING AGENCY
666 MADISON AVENUE   NEW YORK CITY

Mr. Timothy Leary
Millbrook, N.Y.

Dear Mr. Leary

Thank you for your letter outlining methods for bring- ing the United Fruit Company's advertising campaign up to date.

We are sorry to inform you that a cigar company is al- ready using the slogan you suggested, and therefore it would be inappropriate for "Chiquita Banana" to say:

<u>"Why don't you pick me up and smoke me some time?"</u>

As for your other suggestion, although you may be quite right in asserting that LSD is colorless, odorless, non-addictive and most beneficial, we do not see what can be gained by conducting a "challenge race" between LSD and Bufferin to see which gets into the bloodstream fastest.

However, thank you for thinking of us.

Sincerely yours,

Alan Goldman

Alan Goldman
Account Executive

CITY OF MILLBROOK, NEW YORK
DEPARTMENT OF TRAFFIC

Name: *TIMOTHY LEARY*   Date: *11/2/67*

Nature of Traffic Violation: *EXCEEDING SPEED LIMIT DOWN MAIN ST., SMASHING INTO FIRE HYDRANT, CAREENING 6 FEET IN THE AIR, PLOWING THROUGH CROWD OF PEDESTRIANS AND CRASHING THROUGH A DEPARTMENT STORE WINDOW.*

Arresting Officer: *B. Smoot*

Shield No. *784*

Comments by Arresting Officer:
SUBJECT WAS NOT DRIVING A CAR AT THE TIME!

ID Card (in wallet)

NAME Dr. Timothy Leary
ADDRESS Millbrook, N.Y.
OCCUPATION Professor, Lecturer, Mind-Bender, Prince of Pot, High Priest of L.S.D. and Messiah

IN CASE OF EMERGENCY, NOTIFY:
Anybody but the FUZZ! They could never "tune in" on my vibrations!

Jennie:—
Here is the Menu for tomorrow. Please see to it that all items are included, as I have carefully calculated these meals to meet the minimum daily adult requirements.
— T.L

BREAKFAST
Chilled Morning
Glory Seed Juice

Heroin Hot Cakes
LSD Omelette
Morphine Toast
Tea

LUNCH
Airplane Glue Soup
Hashish Salad
LSD Burger
French Fried Hemp
Poppy Seed Pudding
Tea

DINNER
LSD Cocktail
Sacred Mushroom Soup
Marijuana Marinara
Choice of:
"Pot" Roast
"Pot" Pie
or
"Pot" Cheese
Peyote Popovers
Tea

MIDNIGHT SNACK
LSD Cookies
and Milk

Mutual OF OMAHA

Mr. Timothy Leary
Millbrook, N.Y.

Dear Mr. Leary

We are in receipt of your air mail special delivery letter requesting immediate coverage for you and the 23 members of your group in the amount of $250,000 (the maximum) each.

Before we can underwrite such a policy, we will need some additional information:
(1) Would you please tell us exactly what kind of "Flight Insurance" you had in mind?
(2) Do you plan on flying together as a group, or separately?
(3) Is this Flight Insurance for one round-trip, or do you and your group plan on making more than one trip each year? In which case, would you want to be covered? In
(4) How about one-way trips? Will there be any?
Awaiting your prompt reply, I remain

Very truly yours,
Al State
Al State
New Policy Dept.

HARMS MUSIC PUBLISHING, INC.
Brill Building, New York City

Dear Mr. Leary:

In answer to your recent inquiry, the phrase you are referring to is from a Cole Porter song, copyright 1935, entitled "Just One Of Those Things".

As far as we can determine, Mr. Porter had no actual basis in scientific fact for using the phrase, and it is NOT possible to take "a trip to the moon on gossamer wings"!

Thank you for your interest.

Very truly yours,
Norman Blagman
Norman Blagman
Research Dept.

LEAGUE FOR SPIRITUAL DISCOVERY
Sanctuary For Psychedelic Scholars Millbrook, New York
MEMO TO: Dr. Timothy Leary
FROM: Carmine Flippo, Student

Last night, I took my first "LSD trip". You promised me that I would experience breathtaking beauty, divine energy, a spiritual awakening, a sensual unfolding and incredible ecstasy. Instead, all I got was like this tremendous pain in my head. Should I take an aspirin?

CF

Don't be a fool, Carmine! We still don't know exactly how aspirin works, and whether it can be harmful if taken indiscriminately.
— Dr. L.

THE MAD LIBRARY OF

ROCK 'N' ROLL HITS THAT HAVE BECOME CLASSICS

Real Funny Jokes From The Humor Collections of Bennett Cerf

Quality TV Programming—A·B·C

EQUALITY AND JUSTICE IN ALABAMA AND MISSISSIPPI

GERMANS WHO ADMIT THEY BACKED THE NAZIS

Momentous Decisions I Have Made—Dwight D. Eisenhower

The Dynamic Personality of Joey Bishop

The Constructive Accomplishments Of The John Birch Society

My Deep Concern Over The Population Explosion—Pope Paul VI

The Acting Talent Of John Wayne

Due Respect For Justice And The Law—Adam Clayton Powell

WONDERFUL THINGS THAT A NICKEL WILL STILL BUY

HONESTY IN ADVERTISING

MORAL EXAMPLES SET BY AVERAGE ADULTS FOR TODAY'S TEENAGERS

A List Of Doctors To Call In Case Of Emergency Or If You Have No Money

EXTREMELY THIN BOOKS

WRITER: FRANK JACOBS

- A Reading Guide To Best-Sellers With No Dirty Parts
- New York City Taxi Driver's Handbook Of Courtesy
- Gov. Lester Maddox's Favorite Integration Songs
- Political Compromises I Have Made—Senator Wayne Morse
- The Sum And Substance Of My Playboy Philosophies (Parts 1-35) Hugh M. Hefner
- THE ISRAELI'S TOURIST GUIDE TO EGYPT
- The Warm, Sentimental World Of Edward Albee
- THE POLITICAL EXPERIENCE OF SHIRLEY TEMPLE
- Championship Baseball With The N.Y. Mets—Wes Westrum
- Facing The Reality of Everyday Living—Dr. Timothy Leary
- MY PLANS·FOR PEACEFUL COEXISTENCE WITH THE WEST—MAO TSE TUNG
- The Modesty Of Cassius Clay
- A GUIDE TO HAPPY MARRIAGE—Zsa Zsa Gabor
- Making It On Your Own—Nancy Sinatra
- MAD MAGAZINE'S CONTRIBUTIONS TO AMERICAN CULTURE

THE TEN COMMAND

PRODUCED

PHOTOS BY: U.P.I.

I

THOU SHALT HAVE NO OTHER GODS BEFORE ME.

II

THOU SHALT NOT MAKE UNTO THEE ANY GRAVEN IMAGE,

III

THOU SHALT NOT TAKE THE NAME OF THE LORD, THY GOD, IN VAIN;

MENTS - REVISITED

BY: MAX BRANDEL

& WORLD WIDE

IV

REMEMBER THE SABBATH DAY, TO KEEP IT HOLY.

V

HONOR THY FATHER AND THY MOTHER:

VI

THOU SHALT NOT KILL.

VII
THOU SHALT NOT COMMIT ADULTERY.

VIII
THOU SHALT NOT STEAL.

IX
THOU SHALT NOT BEAR FALSE WITNESS AGAINST THY NEIGHBOR.

X
THOU SHALT NOT COVET THY NEIGHBOR'S WIFE.

THERE'S A WILD NEW GROUP OF PEOPLE WHO HAVE BECOME PROMINENT IN AMERICA RECENTLY. THEY HAVE THEIR OWN UNIQUE LANGUAGE, THEIR OWN STRANGE BEHAVIOR, AND THEIR OWN BIZARRE PHILOSOPHY WHICH IS COMPLETELY MISUNDERSTOOD BY MANY OLDSTERS. THE GROUP IS KNOWN AS "MODERATE REPUBLICANS". HOWEVER, IN ADDITION TO THOSE CREEPS, THERE IS *ANOTHER* WEIRD SUB-CULTURE WITH *ANOTHER* SET OF HANG-UPS. THIS GROUP IS KNOWN AS "HIPPIES". THEY'RE *EVEN* MORE MISUNDERSTOOD THAN "MODERATE REPUBLICANS". AND SO, AS A PUBLIC SERVICE—SO THAT THEY WILL BE MISUNDERSTOOD *EVEN MORE* SO, MAD MAGAZINE PRESENTS . . .

APRIL 1968

35 CUBES

HIPPIE

THE MAGAZINE THAT TURNS YOU ON

(. . . if you're cool enough to light it up and smoke it!)

I Turned On, Tuned In, And Broke Out!
The Confessions Of A Teeny-Bopper With Acne

Is Free Love Worth It?

New Gimmick Making The Scene:
LSD On Saccharin Tablets For Diabetic Tripsters

SPECIAL FULL-COLOR FEATURE
42 Flower Arrangements For Your Head

What To Do About God After You Finally Find Him

20 New Middle-Class Occupations You Can Put Down

"I FOUND NIRVANA IN A RENTED LOFT ON HAIGHT STREET"

"What's All This Nonsense About LSD Affecting Our Chromosomes?"
By Samantha Bleeckerstreet, Mother of the famous "Siamese Sextuplets."

ARTIST: GEORGE WOODBRIDGE   WRITER: ARNIE KOGEN

THIS BUILDING IS CONDEMNED

A MOTION PICTURE SO BRUTALLY FRANK AND SO SHOCKING THAT ONLY A WIGGED-OUT PRODUCER LIKE NIRVANA E. LEVINE WOULD DARE MAKE IT!

Psychedelic Pictures Present:

The Wild Freakout Acid Trip At The Hippie Teeny-Bopper Love-In Orgy On The Strip

Formerly Titled: "I Found My Tender Love In San Francisco"

IN GLORIOUS 70mm SIN-EMASCOPE AND STARTLING LSD-COLOR!

Starring

Peter Fonda	Andy Warhol	Paul Krassner	Joe Pepitone
as "Honda"	as "Soupy"	as "The Dreamer"	as "Fungo"

and introducing GOD in His first important role . . . as "President Johnson"

SEE: 10,000 WILD-EYED HIPPIES FLOGGING EACH OTHER INTO INSENSIBILITY WITH THEIR HAIR

SEE: 12,000 SCREAMING TEENY-BOPPERS FIGHTING FOR THE BLANKET IN THE ONE BED THEY SHARE

SEE: 15,000 BERSERK DIGGERS GROVELING FOR A ROACH THAT FELL DOWN A SEWER ON N. Y.'S EAST SIDE

SEE: 8 CRAZY USHERS LEAD YOU TO YOUR SEAT USING A PSYCHEDELIC STROBE LIGHT TO PUT YOU ON

THREE FULL DAYS IN THE MAKING!

FILMED ON LOCATION IN WARREN BEATTY'S RUMPUS ROOM

Recommended For Mature Hippies Only   No One Will Be Seated During The Last Five Orgies

I Had Tried Every Kick There Was!

I Had Seen It All!

And Then...

I DISCOVERED A WILD NEW VIBRATION

by Raga Hotchkiss

I had been one of the original "flower-children". I had put my parents down when I was 2, gone into retreat at 2½, and blown my mind on "LSD-Pablum" at 3.

I had meditated on every mountain, including Mt. Vesuvius—where I'd grooved a minor eruption while shouting "Sock It To Me, Baby!" I had "switched on" and "found my thing" with the great Hippie Philosophers, like Socrates and Nietzsche and Buddha—not only reading them, but *dating* them as well! (I was on uncut morphine at that time!)

I had grooved on STP tabs, tripped on LSD, flown on hashish, smoked bananas, and inhaled the glue from airplanes! Real airplanes! TWA jets! While they were still in flight!

I had even freaked out on the 29th flavor at the Haight-Ashbury Howard Johnson's!

I had done it all! Seen it all! Now, at 15, I was ready for wilder, more mature kicks. I was seeking a brand new trip, elsewhere. And then, suddenly, one day I found it.

Suddenly, one day, I felt this WILD, NEW, FAR-OUT, MIND-BLOWING VIBRATION.

You see, I was walking barefoot through Tompkins Square Park in the rain at the time. I was wearing strand upon strand of those little metallic beads around my neck, and string upon string of those little metallic bells around my feet. And suddenly, there was this ear-splitting *clap of thunder*, like, right over my head . . . and this *blinding lightning flash!*

Before I knew it, I was (CONT. ON PAGE 57)

The Hippie HALL OF SHAME

The Hippies below have been placed on our Dishonor Roll and blacklisted from the following Hippie Communities: The East Village in N. Y., Haight-Ashbury in S. F., Fire Island on L. I., Sunset Blvd. in L. A. and Munchkin Land in Oz. They have turned on to activities detrimental to our movement and should be avoided at all costs. Do not . . . repeat . . . DO NOT feed them or let them sleep in your pad.

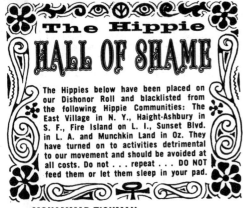

MOHAMMAD TISHMAN
Tompkins Square Park

For burning incense at a suburban barbecue lawn party

GAUGAIN GREENSPAN
Greenwich Village

For coming to a love-in with his own date

MANDALA O'TOOLE
Haight-Ashbury

For smoking a cigarette with a brand-name on it

SAROD COWZNOFSKI
Fire Island

For taking an LSD trip and seeing his parents

ZEN RAPPAPORT
Ocean Beach

For being over thirty years of age

ASK ABBA — Advice To The Up Tight

Each issue, Abba Bennadam answers the questions of the uptight, the turned-on, the freaked-out, the hung-up and the far-mished. Abba Bennadam is a Mystic, a Seer, a Prophet, a Poet, a Free-Thinker and an Aluminum Storm Door Salesman. Abba Bennadam is also a very wise man. Because he realizes that you can't make a living as a Mystic, a Seer, a Prophet, a Poet or a Free-Thinker . . . only as an Aluminum Storm Door Salesman.

Dear Abba:
I am planning to take my first mind-expanding "trip". But I have been warned that LSD is habit-forming. Is this true?
Bugged
San Francisco, Cal.

Dear Bugged:
I have been taking mind-expanding LSD trips every day for the past 11 years, and I haven't found it habit-forming.

* * *

Dear Abba:
Like, I am hip. Can you help me. I am looking for some wild new vibration. I would prefer something relating to the Far Eastern cults. Do you have any suggestions?
Hopped-Up
St. Louis, Mo.

Dear Hopped-Up:
Try sticking your head between two Chinese gongs.

* * *

Dear Abba:
Enclosed is my picture. I am an Acid-Head living on Fire Island, N. Y. Recently, my Doctor informed me that I was pregnant. I have heard that LSD can affect the chromosomes. Since I take LSD trips regularly, do you think that this may endanger my pregnancy?
Worried
Cherry Grove, N. Y.

Dear Worried:
Ordinarily, no. But in your case, Sir, there may be some complications.

* * *

Dear Abba:
I have tuned in on a wild new emotional trip and I think it's wonderful. Instead of the fleeting, impersonal, violent, unfeeling, dispassionate love many hedonist Hippies turn on to just for kicks, when I make love I try to make it into something beautiful and precious and close. What do you think?
At Peace
Greenwich Village, N. Y.

Dear At Peace:
I think that's disgusting!

* * *

Dear Abba:
I am approaching 30, and I still haven't found God! Man, I'm getting uptight over it! How and where can I find Him?
Rattled
Chicago, Ill.

Dear Rattled:
Don't lose your cool. I'll tell Him you're looking for Him the next time I see Him.

Dear Abba:
Last week, I really took a bad "trip". First I saw my body cut into hundreds of pieces. Then I saw my nose under my lip and one eye missing. Then I saw my skin turn blue, then green, then purple. What was I on?
Freaked-Out
New York City

Dear Freaked-Out:
You were on the second floor of the Museum of Modern Art, and that was a Picasso you were looking at.

* * *

Dear Abba:
I've smoked bananas, morning glory seeds, grapefruit rinds, grass (not pot, but "crab"), melons, prune pits . . .just about anything you can name. Now, some cat tells me I can groove with salmon. I think he's putting me on. So, clue me, Man! Ever, like, smoked salmon?
Hassled
Denver, Colo.

Dear Hassled:
No, but I once dug pickled lox!

* * *

Dear Abba:
Baby, like, I'm woke you copped a plea with the fuzz when they strung you out after turning on to boo and grooving with acid in your pad with this out of sight chick who was tripping on STP but couldn't cool it because she was strapped for bread and lacking the universal oom. So I put you down!
Switched-On
San Francisco, Cal.

Dear Switched-On:
Stop talking like a child!

* * *

Dear Abba:
Our teenage son has run away from our Bleecker Street pad and is now living in a split-level house in suburban Larchmont, where he is taking trips in a 1968 Ford Mustang, dressing in the latest "Mod" fashions, and, worst of all, working for money to pay for these things. Where did we go wrong?
Strung Out
Greenwich Village, N. Y.

Dear Strung-Out:
You wigged out somewhere along the line. If you'd provided him with a normal, dirty, loft environment, shown an interest in his free-love problems, and supplied him with the things he really needed, like hashish and STP pills, perhaps he wouldn't have split the scene for a rebellious life in suburbia.

"UPTIGHT" IS A DRY SUGAR CUBE

by Abu Schulz

READER: IN THE WAY OF EXPLANATION FOR THE NON-HIPPIE

"Uptight" means, like, a bad scene. It's when you're hung up, or wigged out, or you can't make it. We all get "uptight" once in a while. Here are some grooving examples of "uptight":

UPTIGHT is . . .

. . . seeing lilies-of-the-valley sprout from the Marijuana seeds you planted.

UPTIGHT is . . .

. . . having the light go out on the "joint" . . . just as it gets to you.

UPTIGHT is . . .

. . . walking along the Berkeley campus and bumping into Gov. Ronald Reagan.

UPTIGHT is . . .

. . . looking around and seeing Bert Parks at your "pot" party.

UPTIGHT is . . .

. . . discovering that the flower you've been carrying in your hand for two months is actually poison sumac.

UPTIGHT is . . .

. . . taking an LSD trip and seeing "The Mormon Tabernacle Choir".

UPTIGHT is . . .

. . . finding out that Toledo Ohio is " . . . where it's at!"

UPTIGHT is . . .

. . . climbing a mountain in Tibet to meditate, and then forgetting what you went up there for.

UPTIGHT is . . .

. . . saying "Sock it to me, baby!" and then discovering it's Mohammad Ali.

UPTIGHT is . . .

. . . discovering the flowers in your hair attract wasps.

UPTIGHT is . . .

. . . carrying the "papoose" on your back for twenty blocks, and then turning around and discovering there ain't no baby.

UPTIGHT is . . .

. . . contemplating your navel while on LSD, and watching as your appendix starts coming out of it.

WHAT THEY ARE SAYING

Philosophical Gems Overheard In Hippie Communities

Omar Ferdlip
FREE-LANCE HEDONIST

. . . upon his return to the Haight-Ashbury scene after spending fourteen months meditating by himself on the top of Mount Shasta in California:

"Daisies have become the major force in my life!"

Shah Bernbaum
PROFESSIONAL HIPPIE

. . . after being stopped by a tourist who gazed at his shredded Army coat, the garland of petunias in his hair, the filth on his bare feet, the spittle on his lips and the mud in his beard—and then asked him what he was trying to prove, just shrugged and said:

"All I can do is try to be beautiful!"

Samantha Gurney
TOPLESS FREE-VERSE POET

. . . after being discovered living in the third floor bathroom linen closet of the East Village Y.M.C.A., and was asked by cops how come she was there:

"Man, everybody has got to be *someplace!*"

Ecstasy Wainwright
FULL-TIME DROP-OUT FROM LIFE

. . . after being told that his father had just been elected President of a giant corporation with a salary of $175,000-a-year, plus a $100,000 stock-option plan, an unlimited expense account, a luxurious $80,000 home and a new company-owned car:

"Like, that's HIS hang-up!"

Myron The Messiah
PROPHET AND FLUTE REPAIRMAN

. . . asked why he had pelted National Guard Troops with flowers during a riot, and then set fire to himself in protest by leaping barefoot into the steaming hot-fat-vats of a Chicken Delight delivery truck, just smiled:

"Look . . . that just happens to be my *thing!*"

Moses M. Stash
UNEMPLOYED RAGA COMPOSER AND DRIFTER

. . . while passing through a typical square suburban community and seeing a well-groomed teenage boy and a modestly-dressed teenage girl holding hands and gazing at each other while sipping sodas at a corner drug store:

"Lord, what is happening to our youth today?!"

Hippie Happenings
What's Grooving Around Hippie Communities
by Charisma Berkowitz
WHO TELLS IT LIKE IT IS

WILD SIGHTS ABOUT TOWN: SAHIB NESBIT drilling a hole in his cranium. He's looking for a permanent turn-on . . . SINAI BOTCHKINS, at a Hindu "happening", trying to quote the Guru with a mouthful of Hashish . . . SAMANTHA SACKS and DESDEMONA TRESS pelting each other with pussy willows, and breaking out in a rash . . . Hippie cut-up RAMA DOUD, trying for laughs by emptying a sack of Farina on SITAR TWEEDY while shouting "Flour Power!" (He didn't get any!) . . . ANGIE THE OX, SALLY THE SLOB, MURRAY THE UNCLEAN, RIVA THE RAGGED and CHICKIE THE FUZZ among the "Beautiful People" strolling barefoot through the scene.

FURD FLACCID is being consoled by friends after returning from a "bad trip". Not a bad LSD trip. Furd went home to visit his family . . . MADMAN MILLBURN, looking for new kicks, tried injecting alphabet soup in his veins and broke out in four-letter words . . . WILLIE THE WANDERER moved from his loft on Bleecker Street and is now living in a garbage can in Tompkins Square Park. And the best thing is he only has to share it with two other Hippies . . . KORAN CALIBASH finally took a haircut. He had it trimmed right up to his shoulders . . . DRACHMA THE DIGGER has made arrangements for starving N. Y. Hippies to receive food packages from Vietnam War Orphans. Good grooving, Drachma!

DIP YOUR PEN IN ACID, and write to the following shut-ins: JOJO BOTTOMSLEY, recuperating in his pad. JoJo tried to smoke a banana the hard way. While it was still in the Gorilla's mouth! . . . Also to RASHA NASHER, who took a double dose of LSD so he'd be sure to make a "round-trip" . . . Also to BABYJANE FLAUM, who got a hernia carrying the papoose on her back. Seems the baby wasn't in it, but her old man was! . . . Also to the 47 Hippies who were hurt in that terrible crash. Their bed collapsed! . . . Also to MARA, MAJA and SHAH, three local "tripsters" who took LSD together and saw MANNY, MOE and SHEMP—The Three Stooges! Man, what a bad trip!

MONK ROSNER, Raga Flute Player is going into retreat to contemplate Robert Goulet . . . NIRVANA NUSSBAUM is planning to run for President on the "Like" ticket. Seems he isn't popular enough yet to run on the "Love" ticket . . . MOGID REILLY is putting the finishing touches on his new book: "How To Live in Haight-Ashbury on $15.00 a Year" . . . Orchids to Raga Rock Composer SCIMITAR BUNNIGER! Not that he's doing such a good job on his music. It's just that he loves to wear them in his hair . . . **ADD TO OUR "LOOK-ALIKES":** NORMA ZILCH, swinging new East Village teeny-bopper runaway from Great Neck, L. I. and ALLEN GINSBERG . . . **RUMOR OF THE MONTH:** Smoking pot will become legal. The hang-up is: getting high will be outlawed!

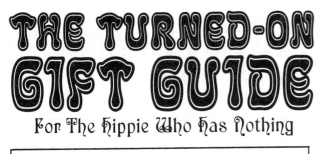

THE TURNED-ON GIFT GUIDE

For The Hippie Who Has Nothing

Do-It-Yourself Tattoo Kit

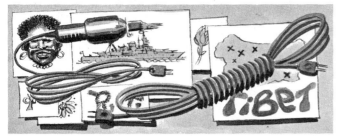

Now you can decorate yourself in the latest Hippie designs —permanently! Comes complete with electric needle, extra-long extension cord (so if you don't have electricity, you can plug it into the lamppost outside your loft), and a huge selection of sample tattoos, including a ¾ view of the Graf Spee, a portrait of a Hottentot Bushman, a full-color map of Tibet showing all of the "meditation mountains", etc.

Fashion Accessories

If you want to be one of the "Beautiful People", then this six-piece fashion wardrobe is a "must"! You get a pair of worn sandals, a moth-eaten Army blanket, a string of beads, a garland of artificial flowers, a live bluebird and a box of real dirt. Can be worn everywhere—in your pad, while making the scene, when meditating on a mountain, or while making a police line-up. You'll look absolutely stunning . . . just like the girls shown modeling the stuff above.

Hippie Collectors Items

For the sentimental Hippie who wants to collect relics of the past. Shoes . . . ties . . . soap . . . bras . . . draft cards . . . combs . . . shaving equipment . . . nylon stockings, etc. We have an unlimited supply of these nostalgic items. They make great gag gifts, planters, ash trays or wall plaques.

My Most Unforgettable Hippie

by Llama Landau

He was out of sight! He was tuned in on the ultimate vibration! He was turned on to the wildest bag possible! He was the hippiest Hippie! He spiritualized everything the true Hippie stands for... peace, love, gentleness and a return to nature. No longer would he pursue the fast buck, or strive for the Madison Avenue concept of happiness, or rot in the suburban-conformist swamp, or support the PTA, or attend the local Church, or kowtow to the Local Draft Board, or participate in Little League. No longer would he suffer the hang-up of the never-ending middle-class drive to produce, produce, produce and succeed, succeed, succeed. He had wigged out on all that!

Instead, he had found true beauty, lasting peace, the inner contentment that all Hippies seek. The true beauty that one enjoys while sitting on a secluded mountain and meditating in the clear, cold wind. The lasting peace that comes after your mind has expanded daily on 500 micrograms of LSD. The inner contentment that comes from eating only pure organic natural foods like liver powder and bone meal and millet.

And as I passed his coffin and gazed down upon his pale, serene face, I realized further that he (Cont. on page 86)

Coming In The Next Issue

"I Got Turned On By Soy Sauce!"
A HIPPIE'S TOUR OF CHINATOWN AND HIS ACCIDENTAL DISCOVERY

A Report On Greenwich Village
"BROTHERLY LOVE'S OKAY, BUT THIS PLACE HAS, LIKE, TOO MUCH, BABY!"

"I Was A Flower Girl At My Own Wedding!"
A HIPPIE BRIDE TELLS WHAT IT'S LIKE TO TRIP DOWN THE AISLE

"I Mixed LSD With Chicken Soup And Took A Trip To Israel!"
(WHICH IS A PRETTY NEAT TRICK CONSIDERING I'M NOT EVEN JEWISH!)

"How To Meditate On A High Mountain Without Getting A Nose-Bleed"

The "Do-It-Yourself Project" Of The Issue:
TAKE THE WORRY OUT OF SMOKING BANANAS WITH THE BRAND NEW
Hippie Magazine Banana Filter

18 Startling Photos of "Bad Trips"
INCLUDING ONE TO PATCHOGUE ON THE LONG ISLAND RAILROAD!

A Hippie's Embarrassing Moment:
"LIKE, HOW I WENT TO SAN FRANCISCO WITH A FLOWER IN MY HAIR ...AND GOT DANDRUFF ON MY DAFFODIL!"

You Know You're REALLY

You Know You're REALLY A PARENT When . . .

. . . you run out of glasses and you have to start serving martinis in "Yogi Bear" mugs!

You Know You're REALLY A PARENT When . . .

. . . the most dreaded event of the year is no longer "Income Tax" time, but that "Pre-Christmas Toy-Assembly" section!

You Know You're REALLY A PARENT When . . .

. . . you discover you're brushing your teeth with "Pimple Cream"!

You Know You're REALLY A PARENT When . . .

. . . you discover that your alarm clock has been broken for five years, and you hadn't even noticed!

You Know You're REALLY A PARENT When . . .

. . . you're asked to solve some "New Math" problems, and it suddenly dawns on you that you never really understood the "Old Math"!

You Know You're REALLY A PARENT When . . .

. . . you never buy anything for the house that isn't plastic, vinyl, or cast iron!

You Know You're REALLY A PARENT When . . .

. . . you catch yourself sneaking a bath with "Mr. Bubble"!

A PARENT When...

ARTIST: PAUL COKER, JR.

WRITERS: PHIL HAHN
& JACK HANRAHAN

You Know You're REALLY A PARENT When . . .

. . . you sit up all night preparing an off-the-cuff, informal explanation of the human reproductive process!

You Know You're REALLY A PARENT When . . .

. . . you suddenly find that your electric bill comes to three dollars less than you paid for batteries for toys that month!

You Know You're REALLY A PARENT When . . .

. . . you find yourself carrying snapshots in your wallet where money used to be!

You Know You're REALLY A PARENT When . . .

. . . you whole-heartedly join an all-out campaign to wipe out those smutty books and magazines you used to read and enjoy!

You Know You're REALLY A PARENT When . . .

. . . you pull the Road Atlas out of the glove compartment and find that its pages have been permanently fused together with Tootsie Rolls!

You Know You're REALLY A PARENT When . . .

. . . the conversation turns to doctors, and the only two names that come to mind are "Spock" and "Seuss"!

You Know You're REALLY A PARENT When . . .

. . . you insult the boss and his wife by leaving early rather than risk losing a good baby-sitter!

You Know You're REALLY A PARENT When . . .

. . . you actually look forward to Mondays!

HAIR

ARTIST & WRITER: DAVE BERG

Much has been written about hallucinogenic drugs like LSD, and the glories (or dangers) of taking psychedelic "trips." Some unsavory magazines have even featured this topic on their covers in order to sell copies. (See MAD #116.) And so, because MAD is interested

A PSYCHED

9:00- I enter the offices of MAD Magazine and I am given L.S.D. on a sugar cube which I put into my coffee and drink.

9:06- My stomach gurgles and my throat tightens. I never use sugar in my coffee!

9:18- A blood-curdling scream pierces the air. I hear humanity crying out in anguish... suffering pain... intense pain! Is it my first HALLUCINATION?

9:20 NO!! It is the Publisher of MAD- Bill Gaines-writing a check! It is the same sound I hear every payday!

9:35 I AM BEGINNING TO THINK THE DRUG WILL HAVE NO EFFECT WHATSOEVERY! HERE IT IS —THIRTY-FIVE MINUTES AFTER GOOBLING, AND NOTHING IS FURNING!

9:53 THE PUBLICHER OF MAD, ADOLPH HITLER, ENTERS THE ROOM AND ASKS IF I AM K.O.? I TELL HIM I'M RASPBERRIES! ON THE WAY OUT, SHE STABS MY TEDDY BEAR! ON PURPOSE!! ON PORPOISE!! SOMETHING IS FISHY!!!

9:76- STILL NO TIGHT! LO I RIP EV

10:10:10 THE T HAIR UN IT'S AN

10:369 HEY! T FLASHI

1492 I S

FI

UZE YOUR ZIPPER CODE!

in truth, because MAD desired to find out once and for all what taking an LSD "trip" was like, and mainly because MAD wanted to feature this topic once again in order to sell copies, we talked one of our writers into taking LSD, and describing his experiences in

ELIC DIARY

WRITER: DICK DEBARTOLO

 CK! MY SKIN IS ON TOO
TAILOR! LOUSY BURTON!
YTHING OFF!!

TOISE IS RACING THE
R MY ARMS!
MS RACE!!!

N'OFF THOSE
BRIGHT LICE!!

LL FEEL
E

RB YOUR
CAR

112:30 THE PLUBISHER OF MUD, HUGH HEFFER, TAPS ME ON THE BROCCOLI—

90:76 I MAKE OUT SHAPES IN THE ROOM A DESK - A LAMP - A STAGECOACH - A PHUNG

1:15 - PEOPLE ARE STAIRING AT ME! I'M A STAIR-CASE! I TRY TO EXPLAIN THAT SOME FUNNY THINGS HAVE HAPPENED TO MY. BUT IT'S NO.

1:30 - EVERYTHING IS BECOMING EXTREMELY CLEAR! BUT IS IT REALITY? DO I REALLY LIVE? OR DO I JUST EXIST IN A CHINGE OF MY BLUK?

1:45 - WHAT IS NOT? AND WHY, IF WE, DO WE? OF COURSE!

2:00 A blood-curdling scream pierces the air. I hear humanity crying out in anguish... suffering pain... intense pain! IS IT AN HALLUCINATION AT LAST??

2:03 NO!! It is the Publisher of MAD— Bill Gaines - writing another check!

2:05 - Everything is back to norbal.

If you've seen it, you'll know exactly what we're talking about! And
If you haven't seen it, rest assured that we've just saved you from

201 MIN. OF A SPA

THE DAWN OF MAN

ARTIST: MORT DRUCKER

CE IDIOCY

Look at that! What is it—a Prehistoric Handball Court!

Who ever heard of a Handball Court that plays music?

Maybe it's a giant-size Prehistoric Transistor Radio?

Or a Dawn of Man Tape Deck?!

You're ALL wrong! It's the mysterious big black thing that's supposed to excite us and make us want to do intelligent things!

Y'know, you're right! I FEEL like doing an intelligent thing . . . !

I feel like QUITTING this stupid movie—RIGHT NOW!!

RITER: DICK DE BARTOLO

Never mind! I'll keep my hand over my mouth!

You'll get used to the little problems . . . like sneezing the same sneeze in and out ten times!

Is that our space station?

I sure hope so! Last month, our Captain tried to land us in the giant Ferris Wheel at Coney Island!

Did you have a pleasant 250,000 mile Express Flight up from Earth, Dr. Haywire?

Yes! We had "In-Flight Movies" . . . They showed us "Doctor Dolittle", "Ben Hur", "Dr. Zhivago", "The Ten Commandments", "War & Peace", "Gone With The Wind", "Camelot"—

You're lucky! On the Local Flights, they show slides of "Sap-Gathering In Maine"!

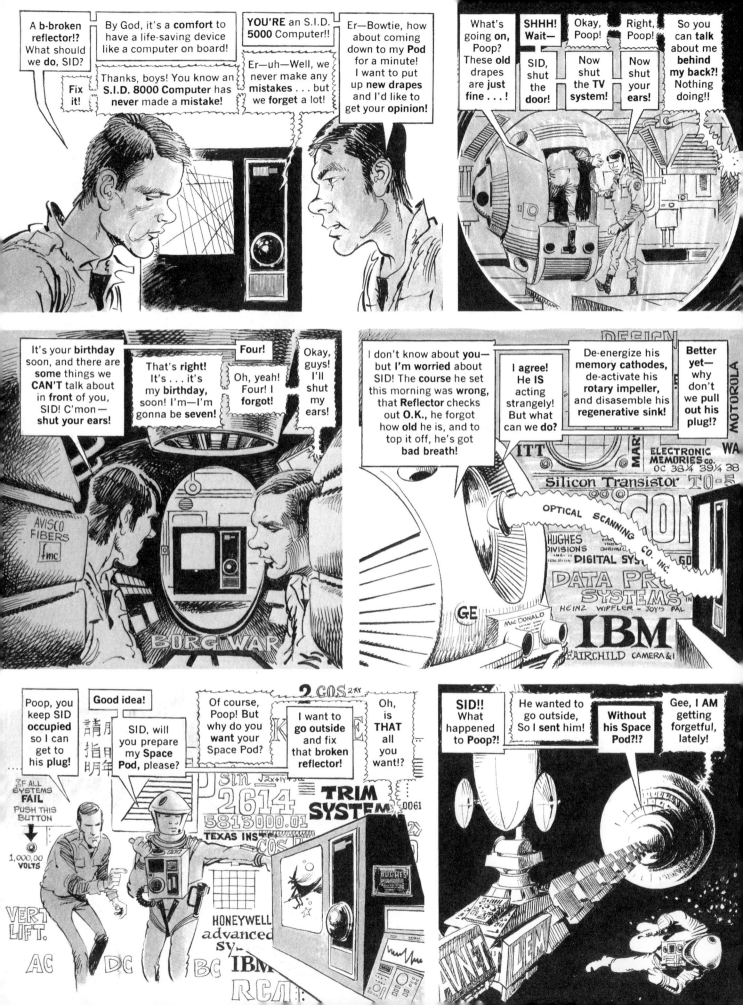

A SAN FRANCISCO TRIP

CONSIDERING THE PROBLEMS THEY HAD LAST SEASON, HERE IS **MAD**'S VERSION OF....

A CBS-TV SUMMER MEMO TO
THE SMOTHERED BROTHERS

ARTIST: JACK RICKARD   WRITTEN BY: RONNIE NATHAN

WHEN YOU RETURN THIS FALL...

Be funny, boys, but don't offend
The sponsor who's your network's friend.
Be funny, boys, but compromise
With those who pay to advertise.
About commercials do not joke,
And cut the coughing when you smoke.
Don't quip about computers, please,
Or ride the auto companies.
Don't laugh detergents down the drain,
Or jest about the aeroplane.
Don't kid the guy who wears cologne,
And kid you not the telephone.
Don't pan the man who's bottle-tanned,
Omit the wit that bites the hand...

Be funny, boys, but don't offend
The viewers on whom we depend.
Be funny, boys, but do not twist
The nose of any chauvinist.
Don't tweak the beak of Bird-man's mate,
Or bait a certain Southern state.
Don't fool around with Uncle Sam,
And stay away from Vietnam.
Keep out of War or we are lost,
Avoid the Draft at any cost.
Recruitment gags we don't allow,
Lay off the C.I.A. and Dow.
Don't kid the Blacks, don't kid the Whites,
Cross out the Klan and Civil Rights...

Be funny, boys, but not too odd,
For heaven's sake, don't mention God.
Be funny, boys, but it's taboo
To clown with Catholic or Jew.
You may not spoof, it's understood,
The sacredness of Motherhood.
Refrain from cracks that might compel
Such blasphemies as Damn or Hell.
Don't speak of sex in your routine,
Remember you must keep it clean.
Refer to breast as chest instead,
And couch in other words, a bed.
When in the course of our employ,
No interjection like "Bolshoi!".
  * * * * * * * *
Aside from that, boys, do feel free
To knock 'em dead for old C.B.

NETWORK PRESSURE

SPONSOR SENSITIVITY

MOBY

AHAB

A MAD PEEK BEHIND

ARTIST: AL JAFFEE

THE SCENES AT A HOSPITAL

WRITER: LARRY SIEGEL

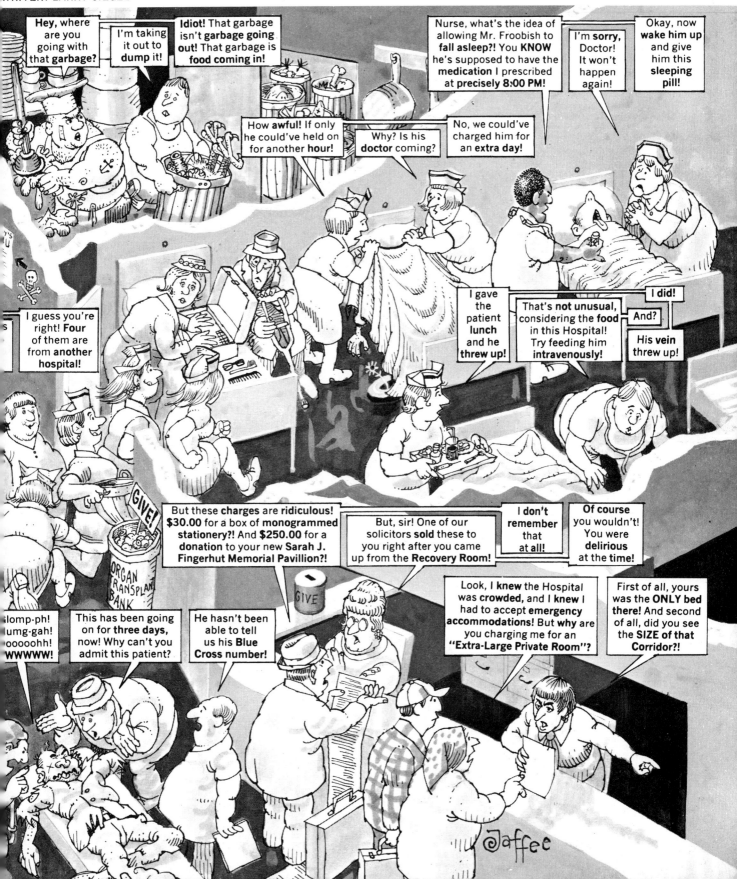

I REMEMBER

THE WONDROUS WOODSTOCK

REMEMBER
MUSIC FAIR

ARTIST: SERGIO ARAGONES
WRITER: FRANK JACOBS

I remember, I remember,
The wondrous Woodstock Fair;
In August, '69, it was,
And all the Heads were there;

Four hundred thousand made the trip,
So Walter Cronkite says,
To groove the Who, the Grateful Dead,
Canned Heat, and Joan Baez!

I remember, I remember,
The traffic unforseen
That clogged the lanes for countless miles
On Highway 17;
And even while I write this verse
I fear there is no doubt
That many drivers still are there
Attempting to get out!

I remember, I remember,
That bleary, bombed-out mass
That wandered 'round the countryside
Freaked out on hash and grass;
Not all of them, I wish to say,
Possessed a glassy stare;
A few, in fact, could still recall
The reason they were there!

I remember, I remember,
That groovy, swinging scene,
That field of wheat that soon became
An open-air latrine;
And how it warmed our happy hearts
And filled us with good cheer
To know the farmer wouldn't need
To buy manure next year!

I remember, I remember,
That cataclysmic flood
Of rain that tumbled from the sky
And turned the Fair to mud;
And how the crowd threw off its clothes
And mingled in the bare,
Until the place looked something like
The final scene of "Hair!"

I remember, I remember,
The way my nights were spent;
The pleasure when I bedded down
Inside my little tent;
And how I found, on waking up,
That all men were my brothers;
That I'd been joined throughout the night
By forty-seven others!

I remember, I remember,
The wondrous Woodstock Fair;
But wait—I haven't told you of
The rock that I heard there;
I'd really like to fill you in,
But much to my dismay,
The closest that I got to it
Was seven miles away!